A Dying Man's Conversation

Last Words on

Life, Success, and Regret

DR.MD.UMAR KHAN

NOTION PRESS

NOTION PRESS

To,

My Beloved Father

CONTENTS

ACKNOWLEDGENTS

With the deepest humility and gratitude, I begin by thanking God, the Most Merciful, whose guidance and blessings have made this book possible. Every word written, every insight shared, and every lesson conveyed is a reflection of the wisdom He has granted me. Without His inspiration and grace, this journey of writing would have remained just a distant thought. He is the source of all knowledge, and it is by His will that this book has come to fruition.

I extend my heartfelt thanks to my parents, who have been my greatest supporters, my silent strength, and my guiding light. Their prayers, sacrifices, and unwavering belief in me have shaped the person I am today. From my earliest days, they instilled in me the values of hard work, patience, and perseverance—lessons that have carried me through every challenge in life. Their love has been a constant presence, an unshakable foundation upon which I have built my dreams. This book is as much a tribute to them as it is a work of my own effort.

To my dear readers, I offer my sincerest appreciation. Writing a book is one thing, but its true purpose is fulfilled only when it finds a home in the hearts of those who read it. You have chosen to spend your precious time with these pages, and for that, I am deeply grateful. I hope that somewhere in these words, you find something that speaks to you, resonates with your journey, and perhaps even changes the way you see the world. If this book offers you even a moment of reflection, comfort, or inspiration, then my purpose in writing it has been fulfilled.

Finally, to every person who has supported, encouraged, or believed in me along the way—thank you. Your kindness, your words of motivation, and your unwavering faith have made this journey all the more meaningful. This book stands as a testament not just to my efforts, but to the love, wisdom, and support I have been blessed with throughout my life.

May this book serve as a reminder that life is fleeting, that wisdom is meant to be shared, and that every moment we have is an opportunity to live, love, and leave behind something meaningful.

Introduction

It is said that life is a series of moments, each fleeting and precious. In our everyday rush, we often forget to pause and reflect, assuming that time is abundant and endless. But there comes a point in everyone's life when time runs short, when the certainty of our final moments forces us to confront the truth about how we've lived, loved, and learned.

This book is built around one such moment—the last conversation between a wise old man and a young man seeking answers. The setting is simple: an old man, lying on his deathbed, and a younger man, sitting by his side, knowing this may be their final exchange.

For the young man, this visit holds the weight of a lifetime's worth of questions—questions about life, purpose, success, and regret. He's unsure of what answers he will receive, but he knows that the wisdom he might gain here could shape the rest of his life.

The old man, tired yet calm, has lived through much—success and failure, joy and sorrow, love and loss. As his body grows frail, his mind grows clearer, holding the distilled wisdom of years, waiting to pass it on.

In these conversations, the young man will ask questions that many of us ponder at different points in our lives. *What is the meaning of success? What will I regret most when I'm old? How can I find happiness and peace in a world filled with noise?* And the old man, through his years of experience, will offer insights that are as timeless as they are profound.

But this is not a one-sided dialogue. The young man, eager to understand, presses for more—questioning, probing, challenging. The conversation flows back and forth, rich with stories, metaphors, and lessons that reveal more than just answers; they reveal the essence of a life well-lived.

Through their exchange, you, the reader, will find yourself drawn into a conversation that transcends time and age. You may recognize your own struggles, regrets, and aspirations reflected in the young man's questions. You may hear echoes of your own life in the old man's wisdom.

This book is more than just a story—it's a guide, a call to reflect, and a challenge to live fully. It reminds us that no matter where we are in life, there is always time to change, to learn, and to grow. And most importantly, it reminds us that the most valuable moments in life are those spent in honest reflection and meaningful conversation.

As you read, ask yourself: *What would I learn if I could have one last conversation with a dying man?* And, perhaps more importantly, *What will I do with what I learn today?*

Welcome to the "A Dying man's conversation".

Chapter 1: The Last Meeting

The soft creaking of the wooden floor echoed through the quiet room as the young man stepped inside. The air was thick with an unspoken weight, a mix of nostalgia and an awareness of fleeting time. The old man lay in bed by the window, his frail frame barely moving, yet his eyes—those wise, knowing eyes—were as sharp as ever.

The young man hesitated for a moment before pulling up a chair beside him. He had visited this room many times before, but this time was different. This time, he knew, might be the last.

"You finally came," the old man said, his voice weak but steady.

The young man swallowed hard. "I had to."

A knowing smile touched the old man's lips. "It's strange, isn't it? We move through life thinking we have all the time in the world. We postpone conversations, assuming there will always be another day. But then, suddenly, we find ourselves at the end of the road, and we realize how little time we truly had."

The young man lowered his gaze, his thoughts tangled with regret. "I should have come sooner."

The old man shook his head. "No. You came when you were meant to. That's how life works. But tell me, what is it that brings you here today?"

The young man exhaled slowly. "I have so many questions, and I fear I may not have enough time to ask them all."

The old man studied him for a moment before nodding. "Then let's not waste any time. Ask me what's in your heart."

The young man hesitated, unsure of where to begin. Then, after a brief pause, he asked, "What is the most important lesson you have learned in life?"

The old man smiled faintly. "We only truly value conversations when we realize they may be the last."

The young man frowned slightly. "What do you mean?"

The old man turned his gaze toward the window, watching the golden hues of the setting sun. "We take people for granted. We assume there will always be another meeting, another phone call, another chance to say what we mean. But when we finally understand that time is slipping away, that's when we start to listen. That's when we speak with sincerity. That's when we finally ask the questions that truly matter."

The young man felt a lump rise in his throat. He had never thought about it that way.

"Then why do we wait until the end?" he asked.

The old man chuckled softly. "Because we are human. We get lost in distractions, in ambitions, in the illusion of endless time. Only when we face loss— when we know something is about to be taken from us—do we open our eyes."

The young man was silent for a moment, his mind racing with memories of unspoken words and missed opportunities. He thought of the many times he had meant to visit, meant to call, meant to ask—but had pushed it aside, believing there was always tomorrow.

Today, he knew better.

"I don't want to make that mistake again," he said, his voice quiet but firm.

The old man nodded approvingly. "Good. Then remember this moment. Remember what it feels like to wish you had spoken sooner. And from this day forward, never leave words unspoken."

The room fell into silence, but it was a silence filled with meaning. The young man looked at his mentor, determined not to waste another moment.

Their last conversation had begun.

Chapter 2: The Illusion of Time

The young man shifted in his chair, letting the weight of the old man's words settle in. He had never thought much about time—not like this. He had always assumed there would be more of it, that life would stretch on endlessly, offering countless chances to do the things that mattered.

But sitting here now, in this dimly lit room with a man who had seen the rise and fall of years, he realized how wrong he had been.

"You said we take time for granted," he began carefully. "But isn't that natural? When we are young, time feels endless. It's hard to live every day as if it's the last."

The old man gave a slow nod. "Yes, and that's the paradox of life. When we have time, we don't value it. When it starts slipping away, we suddenly realize how precious it was."

The young man leaned forward. "So how do we change that? How do we learn to value time before it's too late?"

The old man smiled faintly. "By understanding that every moment is borrowed. Nothing truly belongs to us—not even time. We think we own the hours, the days, the years. But in truth, we are merely borrowing them, and one day, we will have to return them."

The young man's expression grew thoughtful. "That's a difficult way to live. Always thinking about time running out."

The old man chuckled. "It's not about fear; it's about awareness. When you know something is temporary, you cherish it more. Tell me—have you ever held a handful of sand?"

The young man nodded. "Yes."

"And what happens when you squeeze it too tightly?"

"It slips through my fingers."

The old man nodded. "That's time. The more we try to hold on to it carelessly, the more we lose. But if we respect it, if we understand its value, we can use it wisely before it slips away."

The young man sighed, rubbing his hands together. "I've wasted so much time already."

The old man's voice was gentle but firm. "Then don't waste a second more regretting it. Regret is another illusion—it makes you believe you can fix the past, but the past is already gone. What matters is now. Right now, you have a choice: to use your time well, or to let it slip away like sand through your fingers."

The young man absorbed his words, feeling something shift inside him. He had always thought of time as something that stretched infinitely ahead. But now, he saw it differently—it was not something to be wasted or postponed.

It was something to be honored.

"Have you ever wished for more time?" he asked quietly.

The old man's gaze softened. "Yes. But only because I now understand its value. And that is my greatest wish for you—to learn this lesson while you still have time to live it."

A long silence followed. The young man looked at his mentor, feeling the depth of his words settle into his heart.

"I think I understand," he said finally.

The old man smiled. "Good. Then tell me—if time is your most precious gift, how will you use it?"

The young man opened his mouth to answer, but then stopped. He didn't know yet. But he knew one thing for certain—he would never take time for granted again.

Their conversation had only just begun.

Chapter 3: The First Regret We All Face

The young man sat in silence for a while, absorbing the weight of their conversation. The old man's words had already begun to reshape the way he thought about time. Every moment, every conversation, every decision—each carried a significance he had never fully considered before.

He cleared his throat and looked at his mentor, his voice filled with curiosity. "Tell me… what's the first regret people feel in life?"

The old man turned his gaze toward the ceiling, as if searching the vast archives of his memory. A soft smile touched his lips before he answered, "Not listening more."

The young man raised an eyebrow. "Not listening?"

The old man nodded slowly. "Yes. When we are young, we are impatient. We are eager to speak, to prove ourselves, to be heard. We assume we already know enough. But as the years pass, we begin to realize that the most valuable things we could have learned were hidden in the words of others—words we never took the time to truly hear."

The young man leaned forward. "You mean conversations like this?"

"Exactly," the old man said. "Think of how often people speak to us—parents, teachers, elders, even strangers—offering lessons they've gathered from their own experiences. But instead of listening, we dismiss their words, assuming they don't understand us or that their wisdom is outdated."

The young man exhaled slowly, his mind drifting back to moments he had ignored or brushed off the advice of others. How many times had he been too caught up in his own thoughts to truly hear what someone was saying?

"But isn't it natural?" he asked. "When we're young, we feel like we have to make our own mistakes. Isn't that how we learn?"

The old man chuckled. "Yes, mistakes teach us. But wisdom allows us to avoid unnecessary ones. Tell me, if two paths lay before you—one filled with thorns, the other smooth and clear—and someone who had walked both paths warned you about the dangers, would you still choose the thorny one just to learn for yourself?"

The young man hesitated. "I suppose not."

"Then why do we insist on ignoring the wisdom of those who have walked before us?" the old man asked. "Pride? Stubbornness? Or perhaps the illusion that we know better?"

The young man let out a small sigh. "I think it's a mix of all three."

The old man smiled. "And that is why, later in life, people look back and regret not listening more. They realize that so much struggle, so much pain, could have been avoided had they only paid attention."

The young man rubbed his temples, his mind filling with memories—his father's advice that he had dismissed as old-fashioned, his teacher's words that he had ignored in the belief that he knew better. How many valuable lessons had slipped through his fingers simply because he had not truly listened?

"But how can we change that?" he asked. "How do we become better listeners?"

The old man's eyes twinkled. "By listening—not just with our ears, but with our hearts. By being present in conversations, by silencing the urge to respond immediately, and by understanding that every person, no matter how young or old, has something valuable to teach us."

The young man nodded, realizing how much he had to change. He had spent so much time speaking, proving, arguing—yet perhaps the greatest wisdom he could gain would come not from his own words, but from the words of others.

"I will listen more," he said softly. "Starting now."

The old man smiled. "Then you have already taken your first step toward wisdom."

And with that, the conversation continued, carrying with it the weight of lessons that could only be learned by those willing to hear them.

Chapter 4: What Defines a Successful Life?

The young man sat quietly, his mind still turning over the old man's last words. He had never given much thought to the idea of listening as a path to wisdom. And yet, as he sat here now, truly listening, he felt as if he were learning more in this moment than he had in years.

The old man shifted slightly in his bed, adjusting the pillow behind him. Then, after a moment of silence, he spoke.

"Tell me," he said, his voice calm yet deliberate, "are you chasing success, or are you creating it?"

The young man frowned. He had spent much of his life chasing success—working hard, setting goals, striving to prove himself. But he had never thought about it this way.

"I… I suppose I'm chasing it," he admitted. "Isn't that what we're supposed to do? Work hard, achieve more, and become successful?"

The old man smiled knowingly. "That is what the world tells you. But tell me—what does success mean to you?"

The young man hesitated. "Success is… achieving my goals. Building something meaningful. Earning respect. Making a difference."

The old man nodded. "A good answer. But tell me this—do you think success is something you arrive at? A final destination?"

The young man thought for a moment. "I guess I've always seen it that way. Like reaching the top of a mountain."

The old man chuckled softly. "And what happens once you reach the top?"

The young man blinked. "Well… I suppose you enjoy the view."

"For how long?" the old man pressed.

The young man opened his mouth, then closed it. He had never thought about that before.

The old man continued, his voice gentle but firm. "People spend their whole lives climbing, believing that once they reach the top, they will finally be happy. But what they don't realize is that the peak is only a moment. And after that moment, what comes next?"

The young man remained silent, absorbing the weight of the question.

"You see," the old man went on, "success is not a place you arrive at. It is not a title, a trophy, or a bank balance. It is not something you chase—it is something you create, step by step, in the way you live your life every day."

The young man's brows furrowed. "So… how do you create success?"

The old man smiled. "By defining it on your own terms. By understanding that success is not in the reaching, but in the becoming. True success is in the journey—how you grow, how you help others, how you remain true to your values. It is not about standing at the top of a mountain. It is about the strength, the wisdom, and the experiences you gain on the way up."

The young man leaned back in his chair, letting the words sink in. He had always believed success was something to be achieved—a final point where life would finally feel complete. But now, he saw it differently.

"So you're saying… success is not about what we achieve, but who we become?"

The old man nodded. "Exactly."

The young man exhaled, running a hand through his hair. "That changes everything."

"It does," the old man agreed. "And the sooner you understand it, the more fulfilling your journey will be."

The young man looked at his mentor, seeing him in a new light. This man, lying in his bed at the end of his days, was at peace. He had no trophies in sight, no wealth displayed, yet there was a quiet contentment in his presence.

"You feel successful, don't you?" the young man asked.

The old man smiled. "I do. Because I did not chase success. I created it in the way I lived, the relationships I built, and the wisdom I shared. And that, my dear boy, is a success no one can take away."

The young man nodded slowly. He had spent years chasing an idea of success that always seemed just out of reach. But now, for the first time, he realized— perhaps success had been within him all along, waiting to be created.

And with that thought, he felt something shift inside him. The journey had only just begun.

Chapter 5: The Wrong Race

The young man sat in silence, staring at the floor. The old man's words from their last conversation lingered in his mind, unsettling him in ways he couldn't explain.

Success is not something you chase. It is something you create.

He wanted to believe that, but a part of him still felt restless. What if he was too late? What if, while he took his time "creating" success, the world moved ahead without him?

After a long pause, he finally spoke. "I fear falling behind in life."

The old man, lying quietly by the window, turned his head slightly. His tired eyes, though softened by age, still held a sharpness—a deep understanding of things unseen.

"Falling behind?" he repeated. "Behind whom?"

The young man hesitated. "Everyone. My friends. My colleagues. People I see online. It feels like they're all moving ahead—achieving things, buying homes, building their futures. And I..." He exhaled sharply. "I feel stuck."

The old man let out a soft chuckle. "Ah. The race."

The young man looked up. "What race?"

"The one everyone is running," the old man said. "The race to be the fastest, the richest, the most successful. The race to prove something to the world. But tell me..." He paused. "Do you even know where you're running to?"

The young man blinked. "What do you mean?"

The old man turned his gaze toward the sky outside the window. "Most people are running—but they don't know where. They see others running, so they start running too, afraid to be left behind. But they never stop to ask: Where is this race taking me? And is it even the race I want to run?"

The young man frowned. He had never thought about it that way before.

"You see," the old man continued, "life is not a single race with one finish line. It is a journey with different paths, different speeds, and different destinations. But the world tricks you into believing that there is only one race—that if you are not ahead, you are behind. And so, people run. Faster and faster. Chasing, competing, exhausting themselves. And for what?"

The young man swallowed hard. "To win," he said, though the word felt empty as he spoke it.

The old man smiled sadly. "And what exactly do they win? More pressure? More expectations? More fear of losing what they ran so hard to gain?"

The young man looked away. He had spent so much of his life running, comparing, measuring himself against others. He had never questioned whether the race he was in was even one he wanted to run.

"So what should I do?" he asked quietly.

The old man's voice was gentle but firm. "Stop running in someone else's race. Define your own. Walk if you must. Pause if you need to. But move in the direction that matters to *you*—not the one that the world convinces you is important."

The young man let out a slow breath. The weight in his chest, the one that had been pressing down on him for so long, felt a little lighter.

"You are not behind," the old man said. "You are simply walking a different path. And that is not failure. That is freedom."

For the first time in a long while, the young man did not feel the need to run.

Chapter 6: The Greatest Regret of My Life

The room was quiet except for the faint ticking of the *clock* on the wall. The young man sat by the bedside, watching his mentor's frail fingers trace the edge of the blanket. There was a heaviness in the air, something unspoken yet deeply felt.

The young man finally broke the silence. "You've lived a long life," he said softly. "You've seen success, failures, and everything in between. But tell me… what is your greatest regret?"

The old man didn't answer immediately. He turned his gaze toward the window, where the last rays of sunlight painted the sky in hues of orange and gold. His face, lined with the weight of years, seemed to carry a story waiting to be told.

"Not taking a chance when I had it," he finally whispered.

The young man's brows furrowed. "What do you mean?"

The old man sighed, his fingers gripping the blanket just a little tighter. "There was a time in my life when I stood at a crossroads. A moment where I had to choose—step forward into the unknown or stay where it was safe." He paused, his voice tinged with something almost like sorrow. "I chose safety."

The young man leaned in. "What was the chance you didn't take?"

The old man closed his eyes for a moment, as if traveling back in time. "It wasn't just one moment. It was many. The opportunity to tell someone how much they meant to me before it was too late. The dream I postponed, thinking I had more time. The risks I avoided because I was afraid of failing. The words I left unsaid. The paths I never walked because I let fear decide for me."

His voice grew quieter, but the weight of his words only deepened. "People think they will regret their failures. But I can tell you, after all these years, it's not failure that haunts you. It's inaction. The things you *didn't* do. The chances you *didn't* take. The love you *didn't* express. The life you *didn't* live fully."

The young man swallowed hard. He had always feared failing, making the wrong choices, looking foolish. But he had never thought about how much he might regret *not* trying at all.

"So… if you could go back, would you take those chances?" he asked.

The old man smiled faintly. "Without hesitation. Because even if I had failed, at least I would have known. At least I wouldn't have spent a lifetime wondering *what if?*"

The young man felt something shift inside him. How many times had he hesitated? How many dreams had he pushed aside, convincing himself that *someday* would be a better time?

"What if I fail?" he murmured, more to himself than to the old man.

The old man looked at him, his tired eyes filled with quiet wisdom. "Then you learn. You grow. You try again. But you won't have to live with the ache of wondering what could have been."

Silence filled the room once more, but this time, it wasn't heavy—it was awakening.

The young man took a deep breath. He didn't want to live with regrets. He didn't want to be the one sitting by a window years from now, speaking of the chances he never took.

He looked at his mentor, feeling both the weight and the gift of his words. "I won't make the same mistake," he said, more determined than ever.

The old man smiled, his eyes reflecting something close to peace. "Good," he whispered. "Then I have no regrets in sharing mine with you."

Chapter 7: The Weight of Expectations

The young man sat with his head in his hands, staring at the floor. He had come with so many questions, but this one weighed heavier than the rest.

The old man watched him in silence, waiting. He had seen this struggle before—the quiet war between duty and desire, between what is expected and what the heart longs for.

Finally, the young man exhaled and looked up. His voice was low, uncertain. "What if what I want… is not what my family expects of me?"

The old man's gaze softened. "Ah," he said, as if he had been expecting this question all along. "The invisible chains."

The young man frowned. "Chains?"

The old man nodded. "The weight of expectations. The silent pressure to be who others want you to be. To make choices that please them, even if they suffocate you. It is one of the heaviest burdens a person can carry."

The young man swallowed. "But they mean well. They want the best for me."

"Of course," the old man agreed. "Most expectations come from love. But tell me this—who will live your life? You or them?"

The young man hesitated. "Me… but—"

"But you are afraid," the old man finished for him. "Afraid of disappointing them. Afraid of losing their approval. Afraid that choosing yourself means betraying them."

The young man clenched his fists. "Yes."

The old man leaned back against his pillow, his expression thoughtful. "Let me tell you something few people realize until it is too late. Living for others' approval is the fastest way to lose yourself. At first, it seems like a small price to pay—to follow the path they choose, to keep them happy. But little by little, you stop hearing your own voice. You become a stranger to yourself. And one day, you wake up and wonder where your life went."

The young man felt his chest tighten. He had always known he was walking a path laid out for him, but he had never questioned what it was costing him.

"But what if I fail? What if I disappoint them?" he asked, his voice barely above a whisper.

The old man smiled gently. "Then you fail. Then you disappoint them. But at least you *live*. At least you know that the life you are living is your own, not one borrowed from someone else."

The young man's throat felt dry. "Did you ever struggle with this?"

The old man's eyes darkened with memory. "Yes. When I was your age, I had dreams—dreams that didn't align with what my family expected. But I was afraid. So I did what they wanted. I followed their plan. I became what they hoped I would be. And I was… fine. But I was never truly happy."

He let out a slow breath, his fingers tracing patterns on the blanket. "It took me years to find my way back to myself. Years I cannot get back."

The young man felt a deep ache in his chest. "So… what should I do?"

The old man met his gaze, his voice steady. "Ask yourself one question: If you remove everyone else's expectations, what do *you* want? Not what is safe. Not what pleases others. What does *your* heart truly long for?"

The young man closed his eyes for a moment, listening—to himself, to the quiet truth he had been avoiding. And when he opened them, something had changed.

"I think I know," he said softly.

The old man smiled. "Good. Then follow that. The people who truly love you will understand. And even if they don't at first, they will, in time. But you must be brave enough to live *your* life, not the one they have written for you."

The young man nodded, his heart pounding—not with fear, but with something new. Something that felt like freedom.

Chapter 8: The Truth About Wealth

The young man sat back in his chair, his fingers lightly tapping the armrest. The conversations with his mentor had already shaken many of his beliefs, but this time, he felt particularly restless.

The old man noticed. He always noticed. "Something on your mind?"

The young man hesitated before speaking. "I want to be wealthy."

The old man chuckled. "And what does wealth mean to you?"

The young man frowned slightly, choosing his words carefully. "Freedom. Security. The ability to live life on my own terms."

The old man nodded. "And what do you think is the richest thing you own right now?"

The young man glanced down at his watch, then at his phone resting on the bedside table. He thought of his bank account, his savings. None of it felt like the right answer.

"I don't know," he admitted. "Maybe my education? My skills?"

The old man smiled. "Those are valuable, but not the richest things you own."

The young man leaned forward. "Then what is?"

The old man exhaled softly, his gaze drifting to the sky outside. "Your time. Your relationships. Your peace of mind. The ability to sleep without worry. The freedom to wake up and spend your day in a way that brings you joy."

The young man sat still, letting the words settle.

"I have seen people with millions who are miserable," the old man continued. "They have houses but no homes. Money but no time. Luxury but no laughter. They own everything except a sense of fulfillment." He turned back to the young man, his eyes kind but serious. "And I have also seen people with little, who go to bed feeling rich—because their hearts are full, their minds are at peace, and their lives are lived with purpose."

The young man swallowed hard. "So… money doesn't matter?"

The old man shook his head. "Money matters. It gives you comfort, options, and freedom from unnecessary struggle. But it cannot buy what truly fulfills you. That must come from within. Otherwise, no amount of wealth will ever be enough."

The young man looked down at his hands. All his life, he had equated wealth with success. With happiness. But now, he wasn't so sure.

"So… how do I become truly wealthy?" he asked.

The old man smiled. "Earn money, yes. But don't let it own you. Build wealth, but not at the cost of your peace, your values, or the people you love. Because at the end of your life, your bank balance won't matter. What will matter is how you spent your time, who you shared it with, and whether you lived in a way that made your soul feel rich."

The young man let out a slow breath. He had spent years chasing numbers, chasing status. But maybe, just maybe, the richest things in life weren't the ones that could be counted.

And for the first time, he felt like he was starting to understand the truth about wealth.

Chapter 9: The Price of Chasing Success

The young man sat in silence, his thoughts tangled like vines. He had always believed that success was the ultimate goal—the one thing that would make everything else fall into place. But something in the old man's words made him uneasy.

The old man studied him for a moment before speaking. "You look troubled."

The young man sighed. "I've spent my whole life chasing success. Working harder, pushing myself, trying to achieve more. But… why do so many successful people still feel empty?"

The old man's eyes softened with understanding. "Because success, by itself, is just an illusion."

The young man frowned. "What do you mean?"

The old man shifted slightly, his voice calm but firm. "Success is like a mountain. You spend years climbing it, thinking that when you reach the top, you'll finally feel satisfied. But when you get there, what do you see?"

The young man thought for a moment. "Another mountain?"

The old man nodded. "Exactly. The goal keeps moving. The satisfaction you thought you'd feel lasts for a moment, and then... you're chasing again. Higher goals, bigger achievements. And before you know it, your entire life has become a race with no finish line."

The young man felt something tighten in his chest. He had always been running—toward promotions, recognition, more success. But had he ever stopped to ask himself *why*?

"So, should I stop being ambitious?" he asked hesitantly.

The old man smiled. "No. Ambition is a beautiful thing—if it serves you. But if it enslaves you, if it consumes your peace, if it makes you forget *why* you started... then you must ask yourself, what is the price you are paying?"

The young man swallowed. "And what if I realize that I've been chasing the wrong things?"

The old man leaned in slightly. "Then you have a choice. You can continue running, hoping that the next achievement will finally bring you peace. Or you can pause and ask yourself: *What kind of success will truly fulfill me?* Success that feeds your soul, not just your ego. Success that gives, not just takes. Success that lets you sleep peacefully at night, not one that leaves you restless for more."

The young man looked down, deep in thought. He had been chasing success as if it were the answer to everything. But maybe, real success wasn't just about *winning*. Maybe it was about *meaning*.

"How do I know if my ambition is serving me or enslaving me?" he asked.

The old man's gaze was steady. "Ask yourself this—if you had nothing to prove to anyone, would you still be chasing the same things?"

The young man's breath caught in his throat.

He had never thought of it that way.

Chapter 10: The People We Take for Granted

The young man sat in quiet reflection, his fingers tracing the edges of the wooden chair. The room was still, except for the rhythmic ticking of the old *clock* on the wall. The conversation had shifted something deep inside him, but there was still one question that lingered.

"Why do we ignore the people closest to us?" he finally asked, his voice barely above a whisper.

The old man sighed, his gaze drifting toward the window. Outside, the sun was beginning to set, casting a golden hue across the sky. "Because we think they'll always be there," he said. "We believe we have more time."

The young man swallowed. "But we don't, do we?"

The old man turned to him, his expression unreadable. "No. We don't."

A heavy silence settled between them. The young man thought of all the times he had been too busy to return a call, too distracted to notice his mother's tired smile, too caught up in his own world to sit with his father and just talk.

"They understand," he muttered, almost trying to convince himself.

The old man gave a sad smile. "Yes, they do. Until one day, they are gone, and all you're left with is the guilt of not giving them the time you easily gave to strangers."

The young man's chest ached. "Have you ever lost someone like that?"

The old man's eyes clouded with memories. He didn't answer immediately. When he finally spoke, his voice was softer, heavier. "My wife."

The young man sat up straighter, sensing the weight of the words.

"She was always there," the old man continued. "Always kind, always patient. I was busy chasing dreams, always telling her, 'One day, we'll have more time.' And she always smiled, always understood." He exhaled deeply. "But time is never promised. One morning, I woke up, and she was gone."

The young man felt his throat tighten.

"I spent years wishing I could have one more conversation with her," the old man whispered. "One more evening just sitting together. But regrets don't bring people back."

The young man lowered his head. "So what do we do? How do we stop taking people for granted?"

The old man looked at him with quiet intensity. "Be present. Show up for the people who love you. Call your parents while they still wait for your voice. Sit with your siblings before life pulls you in different directions. Appreciate your friends before the years make you strangers." He paused, then added, "Don't wait for a funeral to realize how much someone meant to you."

The young man closed his eyes for a moment. He thought of his mother, who still asked if he had eaten. His father, who masked his care behind stern words. His best friend, who always reached out first.

He had been present for meetings, for deadlines, for ambitions. But had he truly been present for them?

"I need to make a few calls," he whispered, his voice thick with emotion.

The old man smiled knowingly. "Good."

Chapter 11: Love & The Fear of Vulnerability

The young man hesitated before asking his next question. He had always avoided this topic, burying it under ambitions, responsibilities, and the fear of getting hurt. But now, sitting beside his mentor, he felt safe enough to ask.

"Why is love so hard?"

The old man smiled, as if he had been expecting the question. "Because love makes us vulnerable. And vulnerability scares us."

The young man shifted in his seat. "But isn't love supposed to make us happy?"

The old man nodded. "It does. But love also exposes us. It strips away the masks we wear for the world. It asks us to trust, to open our hearts, to risk being hurt.

And most people would rather build walls than take that risk."

The young man swallowed. He had spent his whole life guarding himself, avoiding deep emotions, keeping people at a distance. "But what if love ends in pain?"

The old man sighed, looking out the window as if searching for something in the past. "Then it was still worth it."

The young man frowned. "Even if it breaks you?"

The old man turned to him, his gaze steady. "Especially then. Pain is the price of deep love. But a life without love? That is a far greater loss."

The young man leaned forward, his voice quieter now. "Have you ever been afraid to love?"

A soft chuckle escaped the old man's lips. "Of course. I was once like you—afraid of giving too much, of caring too deeply. I thought being strong meant being unaffected, being in control." He paused, his eyes distant. "But then I met my wife. And she taught me that real strength isn't about guarding your heart. It's about having the courage to share it."

The young man felt something shift inside him. He had always equated strength with independence, with never needing anyone. But maybe… maybe true strength was letting yourself need, letting yourself feel.

"So… how do I stop being afraid?" he asked.

The old man smiled. "You don't. You just love anyway."

The young man looked down, lost in thought. He had spent years avoiding deep emotions, afraid of the pain they might bring. But now, sitting here, he realized something—*the fear of love had kept him from truly living.*

He took a deep breath. Maybe it was time to stop running.

Chapter 12: The Difference Between Real and Fake Friends

The young man sat quietly, his thoughts heavy. He had lost people over the years—friends who once felt like family but had slowly drifted away. Some left without a word, others faded gradually, their presence replaced by silence.

"Why do people leave?" he finally asked.

The old man smiled knowingly. "Because not everyone is meant to stay."

The young man frowned. "But it hurts. You trust someone, you invest in the friendship, and then one day, they're just… gone."

The old man nodded. "It does hurt. And that's what makes real friendships so valuable—because not everyone is willing to stay when things get difficult, when you're no longer convenient, when life changes you." He paused before adding, "Some friends are like shadows. They're with you when the sun is shining but disappear when darkness falls."

The young man exhaled sharply. He had seen this happen. When he was successful, people surrounded him. When he struggled, many of them vanished.

"So how do you know who's real and who's not?" he asked.

The old man smiled. "Time will show you. Real friends don't need constant attention to stay. They don't disappear when you have nothing to offer. They celebrate your wins without envy, stand by you in your failures, and remind you of who you are when you forget."

The young man looked away, a lump forming in his throat. "I wish I had known this earlier."

The old man patted his hand gently. "We all do. But don't let past disappointments make you bitter. Some people enter your life to teach you, not to stay forever. Appreciate the lesson, but don't close your heart to those who truly care."

The young man nodded slowly. "So I should just accept that some friendships won't last?"

The old man's gaze was soft but firm. "Yes. Learn to let go of the ones who leave and hold onto the ones who stay. Because in the end, it's not about how many friends you have—it's about having the right ones."

The young man swallowed hard, feeling both sadness and relief. He had been chasing the wrong friendships, trying to hold onto people who had already let go. Maybe it was time to stop mourning those who left and start appreciating those who stayed.

Chapter 13: Apologies That Come Too Late

The young man sat in deep thought, staring at the floor. Regret had a way of creeping in during quiet moments, reminding him of things left unsaid.

"I wanted to apologize to someone once," he admitted, his voice barely above a whisper. "But I waited too long. And then… they were gone."

The old man sighed, his gaze distant. "That is one of life's cruelest truths—we always think we have more time."

The young man looked up. "Have you ever regretted not apologizing?"

The old man hesitated, then nodded. His voice was softer now, almost fragile. "There was a man I once called my best friend. We built our lives side by side—celebrated successes, mourned losses, shared dreams. But one day, pride got in the way. A misunderstanding, stubborn words, and then... silence."

The young man listened closely, sensing the weight of the story.

"I always thought I'd fix things later," the old man continued. "I told myself, 'We'll talk next week. Next month. Next time we meet.' But life has a way of stealing those chances. One morning, I got the call— he was gone."

A heavy silence filled the room.

The young man swallowed hard. "What did you do?"

The old man gave a sad smile. "I stood at his grave, speaking words he could no longer hear. I told him I was sorry. That I missed him. That the fight was never worth the years we lost." He exhaled deeply. "But apologies made to the dead bring no peace."

The young man felt his throat tighten. There were people he had wronged—some intentionally, some without realizing. And yet, he had let time pass, assuming there would always be a tomorrow.

"What if it's been too long? What if they don't want to hear it anymore?" he asked.

The old man shook his head. "That is not your burden to carry. Your job is to say the words—to free yourself from the weight of regret. Whether they accept it or not is their choice, but at least your heart will be lighter."

The young man nodded slowly. There were calls he needed to make, messages he needed to send. No more waiting. No more assuming there would be time.

He took a deep breath. "I think I have something to do."

The old man smiled. "Good. Do it while you still can."

Chapter 14: The Relationships That Define Us

The young man leaned back in his chair, thinking about the old man's question.

"Who are the five people shaping your life?"

At first, the question seemed simple. But the more he thought about it, the heavier it became.

"Why five?" he asked.

The old man smiled. "Because no one walks through life alone. The people closest to you influence your thoughts, your habits, your choices—sometimes without you even realizing it."

The young man frowned. "I've never really thought about it that way."

The old man nodded. "Most people don't. They let friendships and relationships form by chance, without considering the impact. But tell me—when you spend time with someone, do you feel inspired or drained? Do they push you toward your best self, or do they pull you into habits you regret?"

The young man's chest tightened. He had friends who made him laugh, who filled the silence, who made time pass easily. But did they help him grow? Did they challenge him to be better?

He hesitated before asking, "What if the people shaping me aren't good for me?"

The old man's eyes softened. "Then you must make a choice—continue down the same path, or have the courage to distance yourself."

"But that's hard," the young man admitted. "What if they've been in my life for years?"

The old man sighed. "I once had a friend. We grew up together, shared dreams, built memories. But over time, his choices and mine became different. He pulled me into things that did not align with who I wanted to be. And I had to decide—stay comfortable, or grow?"

The young man leaned forward. "What did you do?"

The old man smiled sadly. "I walked away. And it was one of the hardest things I ever did. But looking back now, I realize it was necessary."

The young man swallowed. He could think of people in his life who held him back, not out of malice, but because they didn't share his vision. He had stayed out of loyalty, out of habit.

"And what about the right people?" he asked.

The old man's eyes brightened. "Ah, those are the ones who change your life. The ones who challenge you, who celebrate your success without envy, who remind you of your worth when you forget it yourself."

The young man nodded slowly. "So I should choose wisely."

The old man placed a gentle hand on his shoulder. "You don't just choose friends—you choose your future."

The young man sat in silence, letting the weight of those words settle. He had some thinking to do.

Chapter 15: The Beauty of Failure

The young man sighed, frustration heavy in his voice. "I'm tired of failing."

The old man smiled knowingly. "Then you're tired of growing."

The young man frowned. "That's not what I mean."

The old man leaned back against his pillow. "No? Then tell me—what do you think failure is?"

The young man hesitated. "It's… losing. Falling short. Proving that I wasn't good enough."

The old man chuckled softly. "That's the mistake most people make. They see failure as a verdict, when in reality, it's a lesson."

The young man crossed his arms. "It doesn't feel like a lesson. It feels like a wound that doesn't heal."

The old man nodded. "Because you're looking at it the wrong way. Do you remember when you were a child, learning to walk?"

The young man raised an eyebrow. "Not really."

"But you fell, didn't you?"

"Of course."

"And yet, you kept trying. You didn't sit on the floor and say, 'Maybe walking isn't for me.' No, you stood up again. And again. Until one day, you didn't fall anymore."

The young man blinked. He had never thought about it that way.

"You see," the old man continued, "when you were young, you understood something that most adults forget—failure is just part of the process. But as we grow older, we let our ego get in the way. We stop seeing failure as feedback and start taking it personally."

The young man looked down. "But what if I fail again?"

The old man smiled. "Then you're one step closer to success. Every failure removes one wrong path and brings you closer to the right one."

The young man exhaled. "It's hard to believe that when you're in the middle of it."

The old man nodded. "I know. But think of the most successful people in history. How many of them succeeded on their first try?"

The young man thought for a moment. "Not many."

"Exactly. Because failure is not the opposite of success—it's part of it." The old man's voice softened. "I have failed many times in my life. Some failures broke me for a while. Some made me question everything. But looking back now, I see that each one was a stepping stone."

The young man sighed. "So what should I do when I fail?"

The old man smiled. "Learn. Adjust. Try again. And most importantly—don't let failure define you. Let it refine you."

The young man sat in silence, letting the words sink in. Maybe failure wasn't the end. Maybe it was just a beginning in disguise.

Chapter 16: The Art of Letting Go

The young man stared out the window, his jaw clenched. "I can't forget what they did," he said, his voice heavy with anger.

The old man watched him for a moment, then sighed. "Who do you think suffers more—the one who hurt you or the one still carrying the weight of it?"

The young man looked away. "I don't know. But I do know it still hurts."

The old man nodded. "Pain is real. But holding onto it is a choice."

The young man frowned. "So you're saying I should just forgive and forget?"

The old man shook his head. "No, forgetting is not the goal. You don't erase the past. You learn from it. But forgiveness—that's for you, not them."

The young man let out a bitter laugh. "And how does that help me?"

The old man smiled sadly. "Because forgiveness is freedom. When you hold onto resentment, you tie yourself to the past. You let someone else's actions control your peace."

The young man's fingers curled into fists. "But they don't deserve forgiveness."

The old man's eyes softened. "Maybe not. But you deserve peace."

Silence settled between them. The young man's mind raced. He had spent years replaying certain moments, certain words, wishing things had been different. Wishing he could change the past.

"You can't change what happened," the old man continued, as if reading his thoughts. "But you can choose whether to keep carrying it."

The young man swallowed. "And how do I let go?"

The old man's voice was gentle. "By accepting that the past can't be rewritten, only understood. By choosing to release the anger, not because they deserve it, but because you deserve to move forward."

The young man closed his eyes. He wanted to argue. He wanted to hold on to the pain because, in some way, it felt like justice. But deep down, he knew the old man was right.

Letting go wasn't about weakness. It was about strength—the strength to free himself from a past that could no longer be changed.

The old man reached out and placed a hand on his shoulder. "You don't have to do it all at once. Just start by loosening your grip. The rest will follow."

The young man exhaled slowly, feeling something shift inside him. The past had taken enough of his life. Maybe it was time to let it go.

Chapter 17: The Ego's Biggest Lie

The young man sat in silence, his thoughts tangled. The old man's last words still echoed in his mind—*forgiveness is freedom.*

But something still didn't sit right.

"So many people hold grudges," he muttered. "They wait for apologies that never come. They stay angry for years. Why? Why is it so hard to just let go?"

The old man smiled faintly, his eyes reflecting a wisdom shaped by time. "Because the ego tells us a lie."

The young man frowned. "What lie?"

"That there's always time." The old man's voice was calm, yet heavy with meaning.

The young man shifted in his chair. "What do you mean?"

The old man exhaled, staring at the ceiling as if he could see his past written there. "The ego convinces you that tomorrow is guaranteed. That you can fix things later. That you can say 'I'm sorry' another day. That you can forgive when you feel like it."

He turned his gaze back to the young man. "But time doesn't wait for our egos to be ready."

The young man felt a sudden tightness in his chest. He thought of all the people he had drifted from, the conversations left unfinished, the pride that had kept him from saying simple words like *I'm sorry* or *I miss you.*

The old man continued, "I once had a dear friend. We were like brothers. But we had an argument—over something so small I can barely remember it now. My ego told me I was right. That he should apologize first. Days passed. Then weeks. Then years." He paused, his voice quieter now. "One day, I decided to call him. I told myself, 'Tomorrow, I'll reach out.'"

The old man closed his eyes for a moment before looking at the young man again. "But tomorrow never came for him."

The room felt heavier. The young man swallowed hard. "You never got to fix things?"

The old man shook his head. "No. And I learned the hard way—*the biggest lie the ego tells you is that there's still time.*"

The young man looked down, his thoughts racing. How many people had he left waiting? How many words had he left unspoken, thinking there would always be another chance?

The old man placed a gentle hand on his arm. "If you have something to say, say it. If you need to forgive, do it. If you need to make amends, don't wait. Because one day, the chance will be gone, and all you'll be left with is regret."

The young man nodded slowly. He understood now. He had been carrying his ego like a shield, believing time was on his side. But time was no one's servant. It moved forward, without mercy, without pause.

And the ego… it was nothing but a liar.

Chapter 18: The Gift of Pain

The room was still quiet except for the soft ticking of the *clock*. The young man sat with his hands clasped, staring at the old man, his mind weighed down by thoughts he hadn't spoken yet.

After a long pause, he finally asked, "Why does life have to hurt so much?"

The old man didn't answer right away. He looked outside the window, watching the last rays of sunlight fade into the evening sky. Then he turned back, his gaze steady. "Because pain is a teacher."

The young man frowned. "But it feels more like a punishment."

The old man shook his head. "No, my son. Pain is not here to destroy you. It is here to shape you."

The young man exhaled sharply. "Then why does it feel so unbearable sometimes?"

The old man smiled faintly. "Because we resist it. We see pain as an enemy, not as a guide."

The young man leaned forward, eager for an explanation. The old man's voice softened as he continued.

"When I was younger, I lost someone I loved dearly. The grief was overwhelming. I wanted to shut the world out, to escape the pain. But no matter what I did, it followed me." He paused, his fingers tracing the edge of his blanket. "And then one day, I stopped running. I sat with my pain. I asked it what it was trying to teach me."

The young man listened, his breath still.

The old man sighed. "And pain whispered back: *Cherish people while you have them. Speak your love while they can still hear it. Because nothing lasts forever.*"

The young man swallowed, feeling something shift inside him.

"Pain makes us see what we once took for granted," the old man continued. "It forces us to grow. It makes us stronger, wiser. Without pain, we would remain unchanged, never realizing the depth of our strength."

The young man thought about his own struggles—the heartbreaks, the disappointments, the moments that had left him feeling broken. He had always wished them away, cursed them for existing. But now, he saw them differently.

"So pain isn't my enemy?" he asked quietly.

The old man smiled. "No. Pain is a gift—one that reveals who you truly are."

The young man nodded slowly, understanding now. Pain wasn't meant to break him. It was meant to build him.

And perhaps, in the end, the lessons it brought were worth the suffering it required.

Chapter 19: The Most Valuable Currency in Life

The young man leaned forward, his elbows resting on his knees. "You've lived a long life," he said. "If you could go back and change one thing, what would it be?"

The old man chuckled softly. "Ah, the illusion of going back," he said, shaking his head. "If only life worked that way."

The young man smiled faintly. "So? What would you change?"

The old man looked at him with knowing eyes. "I would spend my time differently."

The young man's forehead creased. "Time?"

The old man nodded. "Not money. Not possessions. Just time." He sighed. "I spent years chasing things that didn't matter in the end. I thought success was in wealth, in titles, in achievements. But do you know the cruel trick of life?"

The young man shook his head.

The old man leaned back against his pillow. "When you finally have the money, you realize you don't have the time. And when you have the time, you realize you don't have the people you wanted to spend it with."

The young man swallowed. "So, time is more valuable than money?"

The old man gave him a sad smile. "You can always earn more money. But you can never earn more time."

The young man fell silent. He had always believed that making money was the key to a good life. That if he just worked harder, saved more, and built his success, everything would fall into place. But now, he wasn't so sure.

The old man's voice softened. "If I could go back, I'd spend more time with the people I loved. I'd waste fewer moments on worries that never mattered. I'd put my time where my heart truly was."

The young man exhaled. "And yet, most of us spend our time like we have an endless supply."

The old man nodded. "That's the biggest mistake we make. We act like time is ours to control. But it isn't. It slips away, second by second, whether we notice or not."

The young man felt a strange ache in his chest. "So what should we do?"

The old man smiled gently. "Spend your time wisely. Invest it in love, in laughter, in moments that truly matter. Don't trade it all for money, because one day, you'll realize that the richest man is not the one with the most wealth—but the one who spent his time well."

The young man nodded slowly. He had always thought money was life's greatest currency. But now, he saw the truth.

Time was the only thing he could never get back. And from this moment on, he promised himself—he would spend it wisely.

Chapter 20: The Quiet Power of Kindness

The young man sat quietly, watching the old man's frail fingers trace invisible patterns on the blanket. Outside the window, the sky was painted with soft hues of orange and pink, a gentle farewell from the sun.

After a long silence, the young man finally spoke. "Does kindness really matter?"

The old man looked up, a small smile forming on his lips. "What makes you ask that?"

The young man hesitated. "I see people chasing power, money, success… But kindness? It feels like an afterthought. Like something people do when they have nothing else to gain."

The old man chuckled softly. "Ah, my boy. That's where you're mistaken." He paused, as if gathering his thoughts, then continued. "Do you know what people remember most about others?"

The young man thought for a moment, then shook his head.

"They don't remember the car you drove. They don't remember the house you lived in. They don't even remember how much money you had in your bank account." The old man's voice grew softer, more certain. "They remember how you made them feel."

The young man's chest tightened. "But the world rewards ambition, not kindness."

The old man sighed. "That's because the world measures the wrong things." He leaned forward slightly, his tired eyes locking onto the young man's. "Do you know how many times a small act of kindness has saved a life? A simple smile, a word of encouragement, a moment of patience—it can change the course of someone's entire day. Maybe even their entire future."

The young man swallowed hard.

"I once knew a man," the old man continued, his voice distant with memory. "He was a busy man, always running after success. One evening, he saw a boy sitting alone on a park bench, looking lost. He almost walked past him. Almost. But something made him stop. He sat beside the boy and simply asked, *Are you okay?*"

The young man listened, his breath still.

"That boy later told him, *I was going to end my life that night. But you made me feel seen. You made me feel like I mattered.*" The old man's voice trembled slightly. "That one moment of kindness saved him."

The young man blinked, his throat tight. "That man… was it you?"

The old man smiled, but didn't answer. Instead, he simply said, "We never know how far a little kindness will travel. It may seem small to us, but to someone else, it could mean everything."

The young man nodded slowly. He had spent so much time thinking about success, power, and wealth. But now, he wondered—how many lives had he touched with kindness?

The old man exhaled, leaning back against his pillow. "In the end, my boy, you won't be remembered for what you owned. You'll be remembered for how you made people feel."

The young man sat with that truth, letting it settle deep into his soul. And for the first time in his life, he understood—kindness wasn't weakness. It was the quiet power that truly mattered.

Chapter 21: The Problem With Always Being Right

The young man leaned back in his chair, arms crossed. "But what if I *am* right?" he asked. "Should I just stay silent to keep the peace?"

The old man smiled, his eyes distant, as if looking into a past only he could see. "There was a time when I believed being right was the most important thing," he said. "And because of that, I lost a friend I deeply cared about."

The young man leaned forward. "What happened?"

The old man sighed. "It was years ago. A friend and I had a disagreement—something small at first, but our pride made it grow. Neither of us wanted to back down. I had proof. I had logic. I had every reason to believe I was right. And so, I argued. I fought to make him see it my way."

The young man nodded. "And?"

"And I won." The old man's voice was heavy. "I won the argument. But I lost the friendship."

Silence filled the room.

The old man looked out the window. "Days passed. Then weeks. We stopped talking. I kept telling myself, *He'll realize I was right and come back.* But he never did." He let out a slow breath. "And by the time I wanted to reach out, it was too late."

The young man swallowed. "Too late?"

The old man turned to him with tired eyes. "He passed away."

A lump formed in the young man's throat.

"For years, I carried that regret," the old man continued. "Not because I was wrong, but because I had chosen being *right* over being *kind*. And in the end, what did it matter? My friend was gone, and all I had left was the memory of an argument that no longer mattered."

The young man shifted in his seat. "So, what should we do? Just let people believe they're right even when they're not?"

The old man shook his head. "It's not about surrendering your truth. It's about choosing what truly matters. Some battles are worth fighting. But most? Most are just our pride refusing to let go."

The young man exhaled. "I think I've lost people that way too."

The old man smiled gently. "Then learn from my mistake. Before you argue, ask yourself—*Is this worth more than the relationship?* Because sometimes, my boy, being kind is far more important than being right."

The young man nodded slowly, feeling the weight of those words settle deep within him.

Chapter 22: The Illusion of Control

The young man stared at the old man, frustration flickering in his eyes. "How do I control my future?" he asked, his voice edged with desperation. "How do I make sure things go the way I want?"

The old man smiled faintly, as if he had heard this question many times before. He slowly turned his head toward the window, watching the breeze rustle the leaves of a tree outside. "Tell me, my boy," he said gently, "can you control the wind?"

The young man frowned. "No, of course not."

The old man nodded. "But what can you do if the wind changes direction?"

The young man thought for a moment. "I can adjust my sails if I were on a boat... or change my path if I were walking."

The old man turned back to him, his eyes filled with quiet wisdom. "Exactly. You can't control the wind, but you can control how you respond to it."

The young man sighed. "But what about my future? I work hard, I make plans... but what if things don't go the way I want?"

The old man's expression softened. "You are trying to hold sand in a clenched fist. The tighter you grip, the more it slips through your fingers." He paused. "Let me tell you something I wish I had learned earlier—control is an illusion. The only thing you truly control is your choices *today*."

The young man leaned forward, listening intently.

"I once knew a man," the old man continued, "who spent his whole life trying to control everything—his career, his relationships, his future. He planned every detail, left nothing to chance. But then, one day... life laughed at his plans."

The young man swallowed. "What happened?"

"A sudden illness," the old man said softly. "One he never saw coming. It took everything he had built. His career, his stability, even his sense of self. He had spent years preparing for a future that never arrived the way he expected."

The young man's chest tightened. "So what did he do?"

The old man smiled faintly. "He finally understood what I'm telling you now. He stopped trying to control the uncontrollable and focused on what he *could* do—live each day with purpose, make better choices in the present, and let the future unfold as it would."

The young man exhaled slowly.

"You don't control tomorrow, my boy," the old man said gently. "You only control the steps you take today. And if you make the right choices now, the future will take care of itself."

The young man sat back, letting the words sink in. For the first time, he felt a strange sense of peace. Maybe he didn't need to control everything. Maybe, just maybe, he only needed to focus on today.

Chapter 23: What I Wish I Had Known Sooner

The young man sat quietly, sensing the weight in the old man's gaze. There was something different about him today—his breaths were slower, his voice softer, as if he were reaching deep into memories long buried.

"If you could go back," the young man asked, "what's the one thing you would tell your younger self?"

The old man smiled, but there was sadness in his eyes. He looked down at his frail hands, hands that had once been strong, once shaped a life filled with dreams, failures, and lessons.

"I would tell him," the old man said slowly, "that life's answers are simple. Living them is the hard part."

The young man frowned. "What do you mean?"

The old man exhaled. "When we are young, we complicate things. We chase happiness as if it's a destination. We think success is measured by wealth and status. We believe love will always wait for us. But the truth… the truth is painfully simple."

The young man leaned in, eager to understand.

"Happiness," the old man continued, "is not something you find—it's something you create in the small moments. Success is not a finish line—it's in the effort you put in every single day. And love? Love is not about perfection—it's about presence. But we spend years searching for what has always been in front of us."

The young man swallowed. "So why don't we see it sooner?"

The old man chuckled, but it was a sound filled with regret. "Because we believe we have time. We believe we'll *start living* after we get the job, after we make more money, after we achieve something great. But life… life doesn't wait." His voice grew quieter. "One day you wake up and realize you've spent more time chasing than living."

The young man felt something heavy settle in his chest.

"I wish I had known sooner," the old man said, his eyes filled with years of wisdom, "that the best moments of life are the ones we often overlook. That the laughter of a loved one, a quiet evening, the kindness we give—*these* are the things that truly matter." He paused, then looked directly at the young man. "You still have time, my boy. Don't waste it searching for what's already in front of you."

The young man sat in silence, absorbing every word. And for the first time, he saw life—not as a puzzle to be solved, but as a gift to be lived.

Chapter 24: The Question No One Asks Themselves

The young man sat across from the old man, watching as he gazed out of the window, his eyes distant, lost in a place the young man couldn't reach.

Then, without turning his head, the old man asked, "If you died today, what would you regret?"

The question caught the young man off guard. His heart skipped a beat. "I—I don't know," he stammered. "I guess I never thought about it."

The old man smiled knowingly. "That's the problem. No one does."

The young man swallowed, suddenly feeling uneasy. "Why ask something so… morbid?"

The old man turned to him, his tired but wise eyes locking onto his. "Because one day, it won't be a question anymore. It will be reality." He sighed deeply, as if carrying the weight of years spent watching people realize the truth too late.

"When people are young," he continued, "they think they have all the time in the world. They say, 'I'll start tomorrow. I'll apologize next time. I'll follow my dreams someday.' But then… life passes. And when they finally stop to look back, they see a trail of unfinished moments, unsaid words, unlived dreams."

The young man felt a lump form in his throat. "What do people regret the most?"

The old man closed his eyes for a moment, then spoke softly. "They regret not telling the people they love how much they mattered. They regret the time wasted on things that didn't bring them joy. They regret choosing fear over courage, doubt over action." He opened his eyes, looking straight into the young man's soul. "They regret waiting to live."

The young man's chest tightened. "And you?" he asked hesitantly. "Do you have regrets?"

The old man smiled, but it was laced with sorrow. "A few. But I've made peace with them. I lived long enough to correct some, and wise enough to accept the ones I couldn't." He paused. "But you… you still have time."

A silence stretched between them, heavy and meaningful. The young man looked down at his hands, realizing how much of his life he had spent waiting—waiting for the right moment, the perfect circumstances, the guarantee of success.

The old man reached for his hand, his grip weak but firm. "Don't wait, my boy. Live in a way that, if today were your last, you'd close your eyes with no regrets."

The young man nodded, his heart pounding with a realization that would stay with him forever.

Chapter 25: The One Truth That Changes Everything

The young man leaned forward, sensing that something important was about to be said. The old man's eyes, though weary, held a quiet strength. He had spoken of regrets, of time, of choices—but now, there was something different in his gaze.

"What's the one truth that changed everything for you?" the young man asked, his voice barely above a whisper.

The old man smiled—a slow, knowing smile. "That everything you do today will echo in the future."

The young man frowned slightly. "What do you mean?"

The old man exhaled, looking up at the ceiling as if searching for the right words. "Most people live as if their actions disappear the moment they're done. They think their words vanish after they're spoken. But nothing truly disappears. Every choice, every kindness, every mistake—it all leaves a mark. It all comes back in some form."

The young man absorbed this, letting the weight of the words settle in his mind.

"I'll tell you a story," the old man continued. "When I was younger, I met a man who was always angry. He snapped at his family, his friends, even strangers. He never thought much of it—until one day, he found himself alone. His children avoided him, his friends stopped calling. He didn't realize that every moment of impatience, every cruel word, had left a scar that didn't heal."

The young man's throat tightened. "And what happened to him?"

The old man smiled sadly. "He spent his later years trying to fix what was broken. Some things he could, but others… were lost forever."

The young man swallowed hard. "So… what we do today really matters that much?"

The old man nodded. "Every little thing. The way you treat people, the risks you take, the dreams you pursue—they all shape your future. You plant seeds every day, whether you realize it or not. One day, you'll live in the garden you created."

The young man looked down, suddenly feeling the weight of his own choices—things he had put off, words he had left unsaid, people he had ignored.

The old man placed a gentle hand on his. "Live with intention, my boy. Speak with kindness. Chase the dreams that set your soul on fire. Because everything you do today will echo into tomorrow."

The young man nodded slowly. And for the first time, he truly understood.

Chapter 26: The Gift of a Second Chance

The young man sat in silence, staring at his hands. The old man's words lingered in his mind, echoing like ripples in a still pond. He had spent years living on autopilot—chasing things that didn't truly matter, ignoring moments that did. But now, something inside him had shifted.

The old man watched him carefully. "You're thinking about your life, aren't you?"

The young man nodded slowly. "I've wasted so much time," he admitted. "I've been so focused on success, on proving myself, that I never stopped to ask if I was even on the right path."

The old man smiled gently. "Realizing that is the first step."

The young man let out a shaky breath. "But what if I've already made too many mistakes? What if it's too late?"

The old man chuckled softly, shaking his head. "Too late? My boy, as long as you're breathing, it's never too late."

The young man looked up, hope flickering in his eyes. "Really?"

The old man's voice was firm but kind. "Of course. Life gives us second chances every single day. The question is—will you take them?"

The young man swallowed hard. "But what if I fail again?"

The old man's eyes twinkled. "Then you stand up and try again. And again. And again. Do you know the people who truly fail in life?"

The young man shook his head.

"The ones who never try at all."

A deep silence filled the room. The young man felt something shift in his heart—a small but powerful determination.

The old man leaned forward slightly. "If you regret something, fix it. If you need to say something, say it. If you need to change, start now. You don't have to wait for a perfect moment. The moment you decide is the moment your second chance begins."

The young man took a deep breath. He had come here searching for answers. And now, he realized, he had found something even more valuable—a chance to start again.

He met the old man's gaze and whispered, "I won't waste it."

The old man smiled, nodding. "Good. Then go, and make your second chance count."

Chapter 27: The Apology Never Given

The room was quiet except for the soft ticking of the *clock* on the wall. The young man sat by the old man's bedside, watching him stare out the window. Something in his expression seemed distant, as if his mind was traveling back to a moment long ago.

After a while, the young man spoke. "You look lost in thought."

The old man let out a slow breath. "I was just thinking about the apology I never gave."

The young man straightened. "What happened?"

The old man sighed. "I once had a friend—someone who meant the world to me. We had an argument, over something so small that I don't even remember the details anymore. But my pride wouldn't let me say sorry. I told myself I was right and that he should be the one to apologize."

He paused, his wrinkled fingers tracing the edge of his blanket. "Days turned into weeks. Weeks into years. And then one day, I got the news—he was gone. Just like that. And I was left with nothing but the weight of an apology I could never give."

The young man felt a lump in his throat. "Did you ever forgive yourself?"

The old man gave a sad smile. "Some things don't leave you, no matter how much time passes. I carried that regret with me, knowing that a few simple words could have changed everything." He turned to look at the young man. "The heaviest burdens in life aren't the things we did—but the words we never said."

The young man lowered his gaze, thinking about his own life. The people he had wronged. The unresolved conflicts he had let linger. "So what should we do?" he asked softly.

The old man's voice was firm but gentle. "If you owe someone an apology, don't wait. Don't let pride win. Speak while you still have the chance. Because one day, you won't."

The young man nodded slowly, feeling the weight of the lesson settle deep within him. There was someone he needed to call. Someone who deserved to hear the words, *I'm sorry.*

And this time, he wouldn't wait.

Chapter 28: The Roads We Never Took

The old man gazed out of the window, his tired eyes fixed on the fading light of the evening sky. The young man sat beside him, sensing that his mentor's mind was somewhere far away.

"What are you thinking about?" the young man asked.

The old man smiled faintly. "The roads I never took."

The young man leaned forward. "Do you regret them?"

The old man sighed, his voice carrying the weight of years gone by. "At times, yes. There were choices I hesitated to make, paths I was too afraid to walk. I wonder who I might have become if I had been braver."

The young man furrowed his brows. "But didn't life still turn out well for you?"

The old man nodded. "It did. But that's the thing about missed opportunities—they don't always ruin your life, but they do change it. Every decision shapes who we become. And sometimes, the hardest thing to accept is not the mistakes we made, but the chances we never took."

The young man exhaled, thinking about his own life. He thought about the dreams he had set aside, the risks he had avoided, the things he had convinced himself he would do 'someday.'

"How do you know which roads are worth taking?" he asked.

The old man turned to him with gentle eyes. "You don't always know. But if something tugs at your heart for years, if the thought of not trying fills you with regret before it even happens—then maybe, just maybe, that's the road you should take."

The young man swallowed hard. "And if I fail?"

The old man smiled. "Then at least you'll know. Failure is painful, but uncertainty is worse. It's better to walk a road and fall than to spend your life wondering where it might have led."

The young man looked down, deep in thought. He had been waiting—waiting for the right time, the perfect moment. But perhaps the lesson was clear: the roads we never take don't just fade away. They stay with us, whispering *what if* for the rest of our lives.

And he didn't want to live haunted by *what ifs*.

Chapter 29: The Things We Wish We Had Said

The old man closed his eyes for a long moment, as if searching through the memories buried deep within him. The young man watched him, sensing a sadness that had not surfaced before.

"What is it?" he asked gently.

The old man opened his eyes, his voice softer than before. "I was just thinking about the words I never spoke… the things I wish I had said."

The young man tilted his head. "Like what?"

The old man exhaled slowly. "I wish I had told my father how much I admired him. I wish I had told my mother that her sacrifices never went unnoticed. I wish I had told my wife that she was my greatest blessing, even on the days we argued. I wish I had told my friend that I forgave him before life took him away."

The young man swallowed hard, feeling a lump form in his throat. "Why didn't you?"

The old man gave a sad smile. "Because I always thought there would be time. I thought I could say it later, that they already knew. But life doesn't wait for us to gather the courage to speak our hearts. One day, you look up, and the chance is gone."

The young man looked down, his mind racing. He, too, had things left unsaid. Apologies, expressions of love, words of encouragement—so many moments where he had held back, assuming there would always be another time, another day.

"But… if they already knew how you felt, does it really matter?" he asked hesitantly.

The old man reached for the young man's hand, gripping it with surprising strength. "It matters. Because words have power. Because hearing *I love you, I'm proud of you,* or *I forgive you* can change everything for someone. And because when they are gone, the silence of unsaid words will echo in your heart forever."

The young man felt the weight of those words settle deep inside him. How many people in his life were waiting to hear something from him? How many unspoken words were sitting on his tongue, waiting for a 'later' that might never come?

The old man sighed, his voice barely above a whisper. "Don't wait, my boy. If you love someone, tell them. If you're proud of someone, say it. If you need to make things right, do it now. Because one day, all you'll have left are the things you wish you had said."

And in that moment, the young man knew—there were calls he needed to make, words he needed to speak, and hearts he needed to reach. Before it was too late.

Chapter 30: The True Measure of Success

The young man sat in silence for a while, absorbing the old man's words. The weight of the conversation was pressing on his chest, making him question everything he had believed about life. He finally looked up, his eyes filled with uncertainty.

"Can I ask you something?" he said.

The old man smiled, his tired eyes filled with warmth. "Of course, my boy."

The young man hesitated before speaking. "You've lived a long life. You've seen success, failure, love, regret… everything. So tell me—what does it really mean to be successful?"

The old man chuckled softly. "Ah, that question again. I used to think I knew the answer when I was your age. But life has a way of humbling you." He gazed out the window, watching the golden light of the setting sun. "For most of my life, I measured success the way the world does—by titles, money, achievements. I worked hard, earned wealth, gained recognition. People admired me, respected me… but in the quiet moments, when I was alone with my thoughts, I often wondered—was I truly successful?"

The young man frowned. "But weren't you? You built a life for yourself, achieved so much. Isn't that success?"

The old man turned his gaze back to the young man, his expression serious. "Let me ask you something. If I left this world today, and you stood at my funeral, would you remember me for my wealth? For the things I owned? Or would you remember me for how I made you feel, for the lessons I shared, for the moments we spent together?"

The young man's heart clenched. He had never thought about success that way before.

The old man continued, his voice softer now. "Success is not in what you own, my boy. It is in how you live. Did you love deeply? Did you give freely? Did you lift others when they fell? Did you leave the world better than you found it? Because in the end, no one remembers the size of your house, the number in your bank account, or the awards on your shelf. They remember the kindness in your words, the warmth in your presence, and the impact you had on their lives."

The young man looked down, his thoughts swirling. He had spent so much time chasing a version of success that now felt… empty.

"So what should I chase, then?" he asked, his voice barely above a whisper.

The old man smiled, reaching for the young man's hand. "Chase a life that makes you proud. Chase purpose, not just profit. Chase moments, not just milestones. And most importantly, chase the kind of success that doesn't just benefit you, but benefits those around you. Because at the end of your life, true success is not measured by what you had—but by who you were."

The young man swallowed hard, feeling a shift deep within him. For the first time, he saw success in a different light. Not as a destination, not as a trophy to be won, but as a way of living—a legacy to leave behind.

And he knew, from that moment on, he would chase something far greater than wealth or recognition. He would chase a life that truly mattered.

Chapter 31: The Trap of Constant Comparison

The young man sighed, his gaze distant. "I can't help it," he admitted. "Every time I look around, I see people doing better than me. My friends are achieving more, earning more, living better lives. And here I am, always feeling like I'm falling behind."

The old man smiled knowingly. "Ah, the silent thief of happiness—comparison." He adjusted his pillow, his frail hands resting over the blanket. "Let me tell you something, my boy. There was a time when I, too, was trapped in that cycle. I measured my success by looking at others. If someone bought a bigger house, I felt small. If someone earned more, I felt inadequate. And do you know what that gave me?"

The young man shook his head.

"Restlessness," the old man said. "A constant feeling that I wasn't enough. Even when I achieved something, it was never satisfying, because there was always someone doing better. That's the curse of comparison—it makes you blind to your own blessings."

The young man nodded, his mind replaying countless moments when he had scrolled through his phone, feeling lesser because of someone else's highlight reel.

"But how do you stop?" he asked. "It feels impossible."

The old man chuckled softly. "You stop by realizing one simple truth: You are running your own race. The person next to you is running theirs. They have their own challenges, their own struggles, their own timeline. Just because someone reaches a milestone before you doesn't mean you've failed. It just means your journey is different."

The young man absorbed the words, but doubt still lingered in his heart. "But what if I never catch up? What if I'm always behind?"

The old man reached out and tapped the young man's chest lightly. "Behind who?" he asked. "Who made the rule that you must arrive at the same place, at the same time, as everyone else?" He let the words settle before continuing. "Let me ask you something. Have you ever stood at the shore and watched the waves?"

The young man nodded.

"Do they all reach the shore at the same time?"

The young man shook his head. "No… some reach first, some take longer."

"But do they all eventually reach the shore?" the old man asked.

A realization dawned in the young man's eyes. "Yes," he whispered.

The old man smiled. "Exactly. And just like those waves, you will reach where you're meant to be, in your own time. Stop looking at others. Stop measuring your worth through someone else's journey. Look at how far you've come, not how far someone else has gone. Because the moment you stop comparing, you'll realize—you were never behind. You were always on your own path."

The young man exhaled, a weight lifting from his heart. For the first time, he saw life through a different lens—not as a race against others, but as a journey uniquely his own. And that, he realized, was the only race worth running.

Chapter 32: The Myth of the Perfect Plan

The young man sat beside the old man's bed, his brow furrowed in thought. "I just don't know if I'm ready," he admitted. "I want to do something meaningful with my life, but I feel like I need a perfect plan first. What if I fail?"

The old man chuckled, his voice laced with wisdom. "Ah, the illusion of certainty," he said, shaking his head. "Tell me, my boy, do you think I had a perfect plan for my life?"

The young man hesitated. "I assumed you did. You always seem so wise, as if you knew exactly where you were headed."

The old man smiled, his eyes filled with memories. "Let me tell you a secret—no one has it all figured out. Not in the beginning. Not even halfway through.

Life is not a puzzle with clear instructions. It's more like a river. You start at the shore, not knowing where the current will take you."

The young man shifted in his seat, listening intently.

"I once knew a man," the old man continued, "who spent years planning his perfect business. He read every book, analyzed every risk, and waited for the 'right moment.' Do you know what happened?"

The young man shook his head.

"He never started," the old man said simply. "While he waited for perfection, others took imperfect steps and built something real. You see, hesitation is the silent killer of dreams. It convinces you that you need more time, more knowledge, more certainty. But life doesn't wait. If you stand too long on the shore, the river will pass you by."

The young man sighed. "But what if I take the wrong step?"

The old man smiled. "Then you learn. That's how life works. No one walks a straight path. There will be detours, mistakes, failures. But every wrong turn teaches you something valuable. The biggest mistake is not starting at all."

The young man looked down, absorbing the words. "So you're saying... I should just begin, even if I don't have it all figured out?"

The old man nodded. "Exactly. You will never feel fully ready. There will always be doubts. But waiting for the perfect plan is like waiting for a storm to stop before you step outside—you'll spend your whole life waiting."

The young man let out a breath he didn't realize he was holding.

"You don't need a perfect plan," the old man said gently. "You just need to take the first step."

And in that moment, the young man realized—he had been waiting for permission to start. But life had been waiting for him all along.

Chapter 33: The Power of a Simple Gesture

The room was quiet except for the occasional rustling of leaves outside the window. The young man watched as the old man's frail fingers traced the rim of his cup, lost in thought.

After a moment, the young man spoke. "You've lived a long life. You've met so many people. What's the one thing that truly leaves a mark?"

The old man smiled, his eyes distant as if seeing a memory unfold before him. "It's not the grand speeches, the great achievements, or the wealth one accumulates," he said. "It's the small things—things that seem insignificant at the moment but linger in the hearts of others forever."

The young man leaned in. "Like what?"

The old man chuckled. "Like a warm smile given to a stranger on a bad day. A kind word when someone feels invisible. A hand on a shoulder when the world feels too heavy. We are always searching for ways to make an impact, but the truth is, the biggest difference we make is often in the smallest gestures."

The young man thought about this. "But aren't the big things more important? Building something great, making a name for yourself?"

The old man shook his head. "Let me tell you a story," he said.

"There was a young boy who had just lost his father. At the funeral, he sat in silence, too shocked to cry, too young to understand the weight of loss. People came and went, offering condolences, but he felt distant from them all.

Then, an old man—a stranger to him—walked up, knelt beside him, and handed him a small piece of candy. He said nothing, just smiled and pressed the candy into the boy's palm.

Years passed. The boy grew up. He forgot the names of most people who had attended the funeral. But he never forgot that man. That small act—silent, simple, but full of warmth—stayed with him. Because in that moment, it was the only thing that made the world feel a little less empty."

The young man sat still, absorbing the story.

"You see," the old man continued, "we chase after great legacies, but the moments that truly define us are often the ones we don't even realize we're creating. A small act of kindness, done without expectation, can change someone's life in ways we never imagine."

The young man let out a slow breath. "So, you're saying… the little things matter more than we think?"

The old man nodded. "More than anything."

The young man looked out the window, watching the leaves sway gently in the breeze. He thought of all the times he had rushed through life, too caught up in his own worries to notice the people around him. He thought of the strangers he had walked past, the friends he had not checked in on, the small kindnesses he had overlooked.

And for the first time, he realized—changing the world didn't always require something grand. Sometimes, it just took a moment of kindness.

Chapter 34: The Friends We Lose Along the Way

The young man sighed, staring at his hands. "I've lost friends over the years," he admitted. "Some drifted away, some changed, and with some… I don't even know what happened. One day we were close, and then suddenly, we weren't."

The old man nodded knowingly. "That's the nature of life," he said. "Some people walk with you for a lifetime, others just for a season."

The young man frowned. "But why does it hurt so much? If they were meant to leave, why does their absence still feel like a wound that never fully heals?"

The old man exhaled, looking out the window as if searching for an answer in the sky. "Because every person you meet leaves a mark. Some marks are light, like footprints in the sand—beautiful, but washed away with time. Others are carved deep, shaping who you are. And when those people leave, it's not just their presence you miss, but the version of yourself that existed with them."

The young man swallowed. "So what do we do? Hold on? Try to bring them back?"

The old man smiled gently. "No, my boy. We honor them by remembering the lessons they gave us. Some friendships are meant to last forever. Others come to teach us something and then fade away. And that's okay."

The young man leaned back, thinking about the people who had once been his whole world but were now just memories. He thought of the laughter, the late-night talks, the unspoken promises that life had quietly undone. And for the first time, he understood—losing friends wasn't always about something going wrong. Sometimes, it was simply the way life unfolded.

"Instead of mourning what's lost," the old man continued, "be grateful for what was. People enter our lives when we need them, and they leave when their role in our story is done. But their impact? That stays forever."

The young man nodded slowly. He realized that some friendships weren't meant to last a lifetime, but that didn't make them any less real, any less meaningful. Some people were chapters, not the whole book.

And that, he finally understood, was enough.

Chapter 35: The Conversations That Changed Everything

The young man sat in silence, the weight of their conversation settling deep within him. He had come seeking answers, but he hadn't expected his mentor's words to reshape his entire way of thinking.

"I never realized how much power a single conversation could hold," he murmured.

The old man chuckled softly. "Most people don't. But think about it—hasn't there been a moment in your life when someone said something that changed you forever?"

The young man thought for a moment. A childhood memory surfaced—his mother once telling him, *You don't have to be the best, just do your best.* He had carried those words like a shield through years of self-doubt. Then there was the time a stranger had told him, *If it scares you, it probably means you should do it.* That advice had pushed him toward risks that later became his greatest achievements.

"Yes," he admitted. "There have been moments like that."

The old man smiled. "Words shape us more than we realize. A single sentence, spoken at the right time, can change the entire direction of a life. The right words can give someone the courage to keep going or the clarity to walk away."

The young man felt a sudden urgency. "But how do we know when we're having *that* conversation? The one that changes everything?"

The old man sighed, his gaze soft. "We don't. That's the beauty of it. You never know which words will stay with someone forever. That's why we must speak with kindness, with honesty, with meaning. You never know when your words will be the ones that change a life."

The young man swallowed hard. How many times had he dismissed a conversation as ordinary, not realizing it might have been exactly what someone needed to hear?

The old man continued, his voice quieter now. "And sometimes, it's not even about the words—it's about listening. Some of the most life-changing conversations aren't about what you say, but about being present for someone who needs to be heard."

The young man looked at his mentor, lying frail in his bed, yet still offering wisdom that would last long after this moment.

"This conversation," he said slowly, "this is one of those."

The old man smiled, his eyes twinkling with understanding. "I know."

Chapter 36: The Moments That Truly Matter

The room was quiet, except for the rhythmic ticking of the old *clock* on the wall. The young man sat beside the bed, watching his mentor's frail chest rise and fall. He had been here for hours, but time felt different now—slower, heavier.

The old man finally spoke, his voice barely above a whisper. "Do you know what people think about when they reach the end?"

The young man hesitated, then shook his head. He had always imagined that, in their final moments, people might reflect on their greatest achievements, the wealth they had accumulated, or the recognition they had earned.

The old man smiled weakly, as if reading his thoughts. "No one lies on their deathbed thinking about the money they made or the titles they held. At the end, only a few moments matter."

The young man leaned in. "Which moments?"

The old man's eyes seemed to look beyond the room, beyond time itself. "The ones filled with love," he said. "The evenings spent laughing with friends, the quiet conversations with someone who truly understood you. The first time you held your child, the last time you held your mother's hand. The times when you felt alive—not because of what you had, but because of who you were with."

The young man felt a lump rise in his throat. He thought about his own life—the late nights spent chasing success, the days consumed by worry, the moments he had rushed through, always thinking the next milestone would bring happiness.

The old man continued, his breath shallow but his words steady. "When you reach the end, you won't wish for more time in the office. You'll wish for one more dinner with your family. One more sunset with someone you love. One more chance to say the words you left unspoken."

A deep silence settled between them. The young man realized that the greatest moments in life weren't the loud, celebrated ones. They were the quiet, ordinary moments—the ones he had too often overlooked.

He reached out and gently held his mentor's hand. "I don't want to wait until the end to realize what matters," he said.

The old man gave a small nod, his eyes filled with warmth. "Then don't."

Chapter 37: The Cost of Waiting Too Long

The young man sat in reflective silence, the old man's words still echoing in his mind. So many lessons, so much wisdom shared—but one question had been gnawing at him.

"Why do we always think we have more time?" he asked softly.

The old man sighed, his gaze fixed on the ceiling as if it held the secrets of a lifetime. "Because we believe the lie that tomorrow is promised. That there will always be another chance, another day. But the truth is, every time we put something off, we risk losing it forever."

The young man shifted uneasily in his chair. "But sometimes… it's just hard to start. What if it's not the right time? What if I'm not ready?"

The old man gave a gentle smile, his eyes filled with understanding. "I once knew a man who dreamed of starting his own business. He had all the plans laid out, the ideas ready, but he kept waiting—waiting for more money, for the perfect moment, for the fear to go away. Years passed. One day, he woke up and realized that the window of opportunity had closed. He spent the rest of his life working for someone else, haunted by what could have been."

The young man felt a chill run down his spine. "What happened to him?"

The old man's voice softened. "He became a prisoner of his own regrets. You see, procrastination doesn't just delay actions—it steals joy, opportunity, growth. It convinces you that you're safe waiting, but every day you wait is a day you'll never get back."

The young man swallowed hard, thinking of all the things he had postponed—the trips he had planned but never taken, the calls he had meant to make but never dialed, the dreams he had nurtured but never pursued.

"How do I stop waiting?" he asked, desperation in his voice.

The old man's eyes locked onto his, firm yet compassionate. "You stop by realizing that the perfect moment doesn't exist. Conditions will never be ideal, fear will never fully disappear. If something matters to you, start now. Even a small step is better than standing still."

The young man nodded slowly, understanding the weight of the lesson. He had been living in the illusion of 'someday,' not realizing that each passing day was a day he would never reclaim.

"Don't let the fear of imperfection paralyze you," the old man continued. "You don't have to see the whole staircase—just take the first step. Because the cost of waiting too long is losing the chance to live the life you were meant to."

In that moment, the young man made a promise to himself. He would no longer let fear or uncertainty hold him back. He would act, he would move, and he would no longer wait for a tomorrow that might never come.

Chapter 38: The Illusion of 'Someday'

The young man sat quietly, his thoughts heavy. The old man's words had unsettled something deep within him. He had always thought there would be time—time to chase his dreams, time to say the things left unsaid, time to become the person he wanted to be.

But what if there wasn't?

He looked at the old man, who lay peacefully, his eyes reflecting years of wisdom and experience. "Why do people always say they'll do something 'someday'?" the young man asked.

The old man gave a small chuckle, though his voice held a trace of sadness. "Because 'someday' is safe. It makes you feel like you have control, like you're planning for the future. But in truth, 'someday' is just an excuse wrapped in hope. A way to delay action while convincing yourself you'll get to it… eventually."

The young man frowned. "But isn't it important to wait for the right time? To be prepared?"

The old man shook his head. "Tell me, when have you ever truly felt ready for the biggest moments of your life?"

The young man thought for a moment. The truth was—never. When he started his first job, he didn't feel ready. When he fell in love, he wasn't prepared for the emotions that followed. Even now, as he sat here, he didn't feel ready for this conversation.

"I guess… never," he admitted.

The old man smiled. "Exactly. Life doesn't wait for you to feel ready. The perfect moment never arrives. The stars will never align in just the right way. If you wait for 'someday,' all you'll find is regret."

The young man swallowed hard. He thought of all the things he had put off—writing the book he always wanted to write, traveling to the places he dreamed of, telling certain people how much they meant to him. Each time, he had told himself, *Not now. Maybe later. Someday.*

"Have you ever put something off?" he asked.

The old man's eyes softened, as if recalling a distant memory. "Yes. I once loved a woman but was too afraid to tell her. I thought I had time. I told myself, 'Someday, I'll find the right words.' But life had other plans. She moved on, and I never got my chance. I spent years wondering what could have been."

The young man felt a lump in his throat. "And do you regret it?"

The old man nodded slowly. "More than almost anything."

A heavy silence settled between them. The weight of unspoken words, of dreams left untouched, of time lost to hesitation—it was suffocating.

"So what do I do?" the young man finally asked.

The old man met his gaze. "You stop waiting. You stop believing in the illusion of 'someday.' If something matters, start now. Even if it's messy, even if it's small—just begin. Because the only difference between a life well-lived and a life full of regrets is the willingness to act before it's too late."

The young man took a deep breath. He knew, in that moment, that he couldn't keep waiting for the 'right time.' The right time was now.

Chapter 39: The Freedom of Letting Go

The young man sat in silence, staring out the window. The old man's words from their last conversation still echoed in his mind. *Stop waiting. Stop believing in 'someday.'* But another question lingered within him, a weight he couldn't shake.

"I understand now that I can't wait forever to act," he finally said, his voice quiet. "But what about the things I can't change? The mistakes, the disappointments, the things that still haunt me?"

The old man sighed softly, folding his hands over the thin blanket that covered him. "Tell me," he said, "have you ever tried to hold onto something slipping through your fingers? Like sand, or water?"

The young man nodded. "Yes. The tighter you hold on, the faster it escapes."

The old man smiled faintly. "That's exactly how life works. The more we cling to what we cannot control—old wounds, past mistakes, the people who left—the more they consume us. Peace isn't found in holding on. It's found in letting go."

The young man frowned. "But how do you just… let go? Some things feel impossible to release."

The old man looked at him with deep, knowing eyes. "Because we think letting go means losing. But it doesn't. It means freeing ourselves from the weight of what we can't change. Tell me, what is something you still carry?"

The young man hesitated. He had never spoken about it before. "There's someone I hurt," he admitted. "A friend. I said things I shouldn't have. We stopped talking. I wanted to fix it, but too much time passed, and now… it's just too late."

The old man studied him carefully. "Do you think about it often?"

"Every day."

"Has thinking about it changed the past?"

The young man lowered his gaze. "No."

The old man nodded. "And yet, you carry it as if it could."

A long silence stretched between them. The young man's hands clenched into fists, his mind replaying the past like a scene he could never rewrite.

Finally, the old man spoke again, his voice gentle. "Regret is like a locked door. You can stand in front of it forever, wishing it would open, but it never will. The key is acceptance. Accept what was, learn from it, and then—walk away."

The young man exhaled slowly, feeling the truth settle in. "And if I can't?"

The old man gave him a small, knowing smile. "Then it will follow you. And it will steal the peace you are meant to have."

For the first time, the young man understood. He had been holding onto something that no longer existed. The past could not be rewritten. The only thing he could change was how much power he gave it over his present.

"So… I just decide to let go?" he asked.

The old man nodded. "You choose peace over pain. You release what isn't yours to carry anymore."

The young man let out a deep breath. He didn't have to be weighed down by what he couldn't fix. He didn't have to be a prisoner of his own regret.

Maybe peace wasn't found in fixing the past.

Maybe peace was found in finally allowing himself to move forward.

Chapter 40: The Gift of Being Present

The young man sat by the old man's bedside, lost in thought. His mind drifted—back to his regrets, forward to his worries. There was always something unfinished, something waiting in the future to be achieved, something in the past that refused to let go.

The old man watched him for a long moment before speaking. "Where are you right now?"

The young man looked at him, confused. "I'm here… with you."

The old man shook his head. "No, you're not. Your body is here, but your mind is somewhere else. You are thinking about what was or what will be. But tell me, when do you ever truly live?"

The young man frowned. "I don't understand."

The old man smiled faintly. "Life is not in the past—it's gone. Life is not in the future—it hasn't arrived. Life is only ever happening right now. And yet, most people spend their days trapped in places that no longer exist or in moments that may never come."

The young man exhaled slowly. He had always been chasing something—the next goal, the next step, the next version of himself that would finally be happy. But happiness had always seemed one step ahead, never quite within reach.

"How do I stop?" he asked. "How do I stop living in my head?"

The old man turned his gaze toward the open window, where sunlight filtered through the swaying leaves. "Look outside," he said. "Tell me what you see."

The young man followed his gaze. "Trees. The wind moving through them. Birds flying."

"What do you hear?"

He paused, listening. "The rustling of leaves. The faint chirping of birds. Your breathing."

The old man nodded. "For the first time since you sat here, you are actually here. Not in the past. Not in the future. Just here."

The young man felt something shift inside him. A quietness, a stillness he hadn't known he needed.

"The mind is a restless thing," the old man continued. "It drags you to places you don't need to be. It fills you with regret over yesterday and anxiety over tomorrow. But life—life is now. If you do not learn to be present, you will miss it all."

The young man swallowed hard. "So, what should I do?"

The old man smiled. "Breathe. Feel. Notice. When you eat, taste the food. When you walk, feel the ground beneath your feet. When you talk to someone, listen—really listen. The more present you are, the richer your life will be."

The young man looked down at his hands. How many moments had he lost, distracted by things that didn't matter? How many conversations had he only half-heard, too busy thinking about what to say next?

"Being present," the old man said, "is the greatest gift you can give yourself. Because one day, you will look back and realize that the only moments that truly mattered were the ones you were fully there for."

The young man took a slow, deep breath. For the first time in a long while, he felt himself letting go—of the past, of the future. Just for this moment, he was here.

And maybe, that was enough.

Chapter 41: The Lessons That Took a Lifetime to Learn

The old man lay still, his breaths slow but steady. The young man sat beside him, sensing the weight of the moment. This conversation felt different—he could tell the old man was gathering his final words, the ones that mattered most.

"Tell me," the young man asked softly, "if you could go back and teach your younger self everything you've learned… what would you say?"

The old man smiled faintly. "Ah," he whispered, "but that's the thing about wisdom—it cannot be given, only earned."

The young man frowned. "What do you mean?"

The old man sighed, his voice softer now. "Wisdom is not in books or advice. It is in mistakes, in failures, in moments of pain that force you to see life differently. I could tell you what I have learned, but you will only truly understand when life teaches you in its own way."

The young man leaned forward, eager. "Then tell me anyway. Maybe I can learn without making the same mistakes."

The old man chuckled weakly. "If only it worked that way." He closed his eyes for a moment, gathering his thoughts. Then, he began.

"First," he said, "nothing lasts forever—not success, not failure, not pain, not joy. If you cling too tightly to anything, you will suffer."

The young man nodded, absorbing the words.

"Second," the old man continued, "people are not as concerned about you as you think. You spend years worrying about their opinions, but in the end, everyone is too busy living their own life to judge yours for long."

The young man felt a weight lift off his shoulders.

"Third," the old man said, his gaze growing distant, "the things you chase will often disappoint you. The job, the money, the recognition—you think they will make you whole, but they won't. True fulfillment comes from what you give, not what you gain."

The young man looked down, reflecting on his own ambitions.

"Fourth," the old man continued, "you will hurt people, and people will hurt you. But the sooner you learn to forgive—yourself and others—the lighter your heart will be."

The young man swallowed hard. He thought of old grudges, apologies left unsaid.

"And lastly," the old man whispered, "one day, you will run out of time. That is the only certainty in life. So, love deeply. Speak your heart. Take the risk. Live in a way that, when the end comes, you can close your eyes without regret."

Silence filled the room. The young man felt tears sting his eyes. He had asked for wisdom, and now, he felt the depth of it—not just in the words, but in the life behind them.

The old man reached out, his frail hand resting over the young man's. "You will learn all these things, in your own time, in your own way. Just promise me one thing."

The young man gripped his hand. "Anything."

The old man's voice was barely above a whisper. "Don't wait until the end to understand what truly matters."

The young man held his breath, letting the words settle deep in his soul.

And in that moment, he understood—some lessons take a lifetime to learn, but the wisest choice is to live by them before it's too late.

Chapter 42: The Fear That Holds Us Back

The young man sat in silence, staring at his mentor, who lay weak but still wise, his eyes reflecting years of understanding.

"I have a confession," the young man finally said. "There are things I've always wanted to do, but I keep holding myself back. I tell myself I'm not ready, that I'll fail, that I don't have what it takes."

The old man gave a knowing smile. "Fear," he said. "The invisible chain that keeps people from living the life they truly want."

The young man nodded. "How do I get rid of it?"

The old man sighed, looking out of the window as if searching for an answer in the fading light. "Fear never truly disappears," he said. "It lingers in the corners of your mind, whispering doubts, making excuses sound reasonable. The mistake people make is waiting for fear to leave before they take action. But that day never comes."

The young man frowned. "Then what do I do?"

"You move forward despite it," the old man said. "Fear fades when you walk straight through it. Every time you take a step, it weakens. Every time you push past hesitation, it loses its grip. But if you keep waiting to feel 'ready,' you'll wait forever."

The young man swallowed. "But what if I fail?"

The old man chuckled softly. "You will. We all do. But failure isn't the enemy—stagnation is. The real tragedy isn't falling; it's never climbing in the first place."

The room fell quiet for a moment. Then, the young man asked, "Did fear ever hold you back?"

The old man's eyes darkened with memory. "Yes," he admitted. "There was a time when I let fear decide for me. I stayed silent when I should have spoken. I stayed still when I should have moved. And those are the moments I regret most—not the ones where I failed, but the ones where I never tried."

The young man felt a chill run through him. "So the only way to beat fear is to act despite it?"

The old man nodded. "Exactly. Fear is nothing more than an illusion. It only has power if you obey it. But the moment you step forward, even with trembling hands and an uncertain heart, fear begins to lose its control."

The young man inhaled deeply. He had spent years letting fear dictate his choices. But now, he saw it differently. Fear was not a stop sign—it was a test. A test he had to walk through.

The old man smiled. "Courage isn't the absence of fear, my boy. It's choosing to move forward anyway."

Chapter 43: The Stories We Tell Ourselves

The young man sat quietly, his thoughts tangled in uncertainty. "You know," he finally said, "sometimes I feel like no matter what I do, I'll never be good enough."

The old man studied him for a moment before asking, "Who told you that?"

The young man hesitated. "No one. It's just... how I've always felt."

The old man nodded knowingly. "Ah, the stories we tell ourselves."

The young man frowned. "Stories?"

"Yes," the old man said. "Every person carries an inner story—a quiet voice shaping how they see themselves, their potential, and their place in the world. And the danger is, if you repeat a story long enough, it becomes your truth."

The young man leaned forward. "You're saying I created this feeling?"

The old man smiled. "Not consciously. Sometimes, these stories begin when we're young. A single failure convinces us we're not capable. A single rejection makes us believe we're unworthy. A single moment of being overlooked convinces us we're invisible. And before we know it, these moments turn into a narrative—one we live by, whether it's true or not."

The young man swallowed hard. "Then how do I change it?"

The old man's voice was gentle but firm. "You start by questioning it. When you hear that voice saying, 'I'm not good enough,' ask yourself—where is the proof? Who decided this? Is it truly my voice, or did I pick it up from someone else's doubt, someone else's fear?"

The young man's mind raced. How many times had he told himself he wasn't smart enough, strong enough, or worthy enough? And how many times had he never questioned it?

"You see," the old man continued, "the difference between those who rise and those who remain stuck is not intelligence or talent—it's the story they choose to believe. Those who succeed tell themselves a different story. Not a perfect one, but one where failure is a lesson, where struggles are steps, where worth is not measured by others' approval."

The young man exhaled. "So, if I want to change my life, I have to change my story?"

The old man smiled. "Yes. Because the words you whisper to yourself every day shape the reality you live in."

For the first time, the young man saw his past doubts in a different light. They were not unchangeable truths—just old stories waiting to be rewritten.

Chapter 44: The Myth of 'Enough Time'

The young man stared out the window, his fingers tapping restlessly on the arm of his chair. "I have so many things I want to do," he said. "But I feel like I need to wait for the right time."

The old man chuckled softly. "And when will that be?"

The young man hesitated. "I don't know… when I have more experience, more confidence, more money. When I feel ready."

The old man shook his head. "Ah, the myth of 'enough time.' The illusion that tomorrow will always be waiting for us, that one day we'll wake up and everything will align perfectly before we take action." He sighed. "Do you know the greatest thief in life?"

The young man looked at him curiously.

The old man's voice turned solemn. "The idea that you have more time than you do."

The young man swallowed. "But what if I'm not ready?"

The old man's eyes softened. "No one ever is. No one ever feels fully prepared. But the difference between those who succeed and those who don't is simple—some start despite the fear, while others keep waiting for a day that never comes."

The young man leaned back, processing the weight of the words. "So, you're saying I should just begin, even if I don't feel ready?"

The old man nodded. "Yes. Start before you're ready. Take the first step, and clarity will follow. Waiting for the perfect moment is how most dreams die—because perfection never arrives. Time moves, whether we do or not."

A heavy silence filled the room. The young man thought of all the things he had postponed—writing, traveling, learning something new, telling certain people how he truly felt. He had always told himself, *someday*. But what if *someday* never came?

He looked up at the old man. "What's something you waited too long for?"

The old man's gaze drifted to the ceiling, as if searching through the years. "Telling someone I loved them," he finally said. "By the time I was ready, they were gone."

A lump formed in the young man's throat.

The old man turned to him. "Don't make the same mistake. If something matters to you, do it now. Time is only generous to those who don't take it for granted."

The young man nodded slowly, understanding in a way he never had before. He had been waiting for time. But now, he realized—time had been waiting for him.

Chapter 45: The Regret of Wasted Potential

The young man sat quietly, his mind heavy with thoughts. He had always felt he was capable of more, but something had held him back—fear, doubt, or maybe just the comfort of the familiar.

Sensing his silence, the old man spoke, his voice gentle but firm. "Do you know what haunts people the most at the end of their lives?"

The young man shook his head.

"It's not the mistakes they made," the old man said. "It's the things they never did. The talents they never used. The potential they let waste away."

The young man swallowed hard. "But what if I fail?"

The old man smiled. "Failure is not the worst thing. Regret is." He shifted slightly on the bed, his gaze steady. "I've seen brilliant minds play it safe. I've seen talented souls let fear silence them. And I've seen people with gifts so rare, so beautiful—yet they never shared them with the world. Not because they couldn't... but because they didn't."

The young man exhaled, his chest tightening. "What stopped them?"

"The same thing that stops most people," the old man said. "Self-doubt. Procrastination. The belief that they have more time. Or that someone else is more deserving, more capable. But do you know the real tragedy?"

The young man leaned in.

"They never realized that their gifts weren't given to them for themselves. They were meant to share them with the world. And when they didn't... the world lost something precious."

A deep silence settled between them. The young man thought of the ideas he had buried, the passions he had ignored, the excuses he had made.

"What if I don't know what my gift is?" he asked softly.

The old man's eyes sparkled. "Then start exploring. Try, fail, learn. The worst thing you can do is sit and

156

wait for it to be obvious. Talent is discovered through action, not hesitation."

The young man looked down at his hands. "And if I feel I'm not good enough?"

The old man chuckled. "No one starts off great. But even an unpolished gift is more valuable than one that stays hidden forever." He sighed. "At the end of life, we don't regret the things we tried and failed at. We regret the things we never gave ourselves the chance to succeed in."

The young man felt a shift inside him—something deep and undeniable. He had spent too much time holding back, waiting, hesitating. But the thought of leaving his potential unrealized, of carrying his unused talents to the grave, terrified him more than failure ever could.

He looked up, determination settling in his eyes. "I don't want to waste my gifts."

The old man smiled. "Then don't."

Chapter 46: The Love We Fail to Express

The young man stared out the window, watching the sky shift from soft orange to deep blue. He had always believed there would be more time—more moments to say the things he felt but never spoke. But now, sitting beside the old man, he wasn't so sure.

"I wish I had said 'I love you' more often," the old man murmured, his voice distant, as if he were speaking to ghosts of the past.

The young man turned to him. "To whom?"

The old man sighed, his fingers lightly tapping the blanket draped over him. "To my mother before she took her last breath. To my father, who worked tirelessly but never heard those words from me. To my wife, who always understood, yet deserved to hear

158

it more. And to my children, who grew up faster than I realized."

The young man swallowed hard. He thought of his own parents, his siblings, his friends. He loved them—deeply—but when was the last time he had actually said it?

"Why didn't you?" he asked, his voice barely above a whisper.

The old man gave a sad smile. "Pride. Assumption. Thinking they already knew. And sometimes… just waiting for the 'right moment.'" He paused. "But the truth is, there's never a perfect moment. There's just now."

The room fell into silence, heavy with unspoken words and unsent goodbyes.

The young man clenched his fists. "What if it feels awkward? What if they don't say it back?"

The old man chuckled softly. "Love is not a transaction. It's not about hearing it in return. It's about making sure they know." His eyes glistened with a quiet sorrow. "Do you know how many people walk around carrying the weight of words they wish they had said? Do you know how many regret not picking up the phone, not writing the letter, not holding on for just a second longer?"

The young man looked away, ashamed. He had been guilty of this—of assuming people would always be there, of thinking he had more time.

The old man reached for his hand, his grip weak but firm. "Don't wait, my boy. Say it while you still can. To your parents, to your siblings, to your friends. Even to yourself."

The young man nodded, his throat tight. He made a silent vow to never leave love unspoken again.

Chapter 47: The Strength in Asking for Help

The young man had always believed that strength meant standing alone. He prided himself on solving his own problems, carrying his burdens without complaint. But as he sat beside the old man, he saw something in his mentor's tired eyes—a wisdom that came from years of learning what truly mattered.

"You look troubled," the old man observed, his voice gentle.

The young man hesitated before speaking. "I don't like asking for help. It makes me feel weak."

A soft chuckle escaped the old man's lips. "Weak?" He shook his head. "Tell me, have you ever seen a tree standing alone in a storm?"

The young man frowned. "It would break."

"Exactly." The old man gestured to the window, where trees swayed in the wind, their branches intertwined. "The strongest trees grow in forests, their roots connected beneath the earth. They hold each other up. That's how they survive."

The young man exhaled, his shoulders slumping. "But people respect those who do everything on their own."

The old man smiled knowingly. "Do they? Or do they admire those who are honest about their struggles? Those who trust others enough to say, 'I can't do this alone'?"

The young man remained silent, his mind turning over the old man's words.

"Let me tell you something, my boy," the old man continued. "There was a time in my life when I thought just like you. I believed I had to be strong for everyone else, that asking for help would make me a burden." His gaze softened. "But when I finally let people in—when I leaned on my loved ones—I found a strength I never knew existed."

The young man looked down at his hands. "But what if people judge me?"

The old man reached out, his frail fingers resting on the young man's arm. "The right people won't. And those who do? They were never truly there for you to begin with."

The room fell into a comfortable silence.

The young man took a deep breath. For the first time, he wondered if strength wasn't about standing alone—but about knowing when to reach for a hand that was already extended.

Chapter 48: The Beauty of Simple Moments

The young man sat quietly by the old man's bedside, watching the golden light of the evening sun spill through the window. Outside, the leaves rustled gently in the wind, and somewhere in the distance, the laughter of children echoed through the air.

The old man closed his eyes for a moment, breathing deeply. "You know," he said, his voice soft, "the older I get, the more I realize that happiness isn't in the big things we chase."

The young man leaned forward. "Then where is it?"

The old man opened his eyes and smiled. "It's in moments like this."

The young man frowned. "But this is just… a quiet evening."

The old man chuckled. "Exactly."

Seeing the confusion on the young man's face, the old man continued, "I spent years chasing success, thinking happiness was in achievements, wealth, and recognition. But now, when I look back, do you know what I miss the most?"

The young man shook his head.

"The simple moments," the old man said with a sigh. "The quiet tea shared with a friend. The way my mother's hands smelled of flour when she made bread. The sound of my father's voice calling my name. The way the air felt on a walk after the rain."

The young man thought about his own life—about the times he had rushed through days, thinking happiness was always somewhere ahead, waiting to be reached.

"But we don't realize their value in the moment," he admitted.

The old man nodded. "That's the tragedy of life. We are so busy chasing what we think will make us happy that we overlook the happiness already surrounding us."

The young man was silent, his mind replaying memories—late-night talks with his best friend, the warmth of his mother's hug, the scent of old books in his grandfather's study. Moments that had come and gone, unnoticed in their simplicity, yet holding a depth he had never appreciated before.

"How do I start noticing them?" he finally asked.

The old man smiled. "Pause. Breathe. Look around. Let yourself feel." He turned his head slightly toward the window, his voice barely above a whisper. "One day, you'll realize those simple moments were the ones that made life beautiful."

The young man swallowed the lump in his throat. He had spent so much time searching for happiness that he had forgotten to live it.

And for the first time in a long time, he simply sat still—listening, watching, feeling—letting the moment sink in.

Chapter 49: The Lies We Believe About Happiness

The young man sat in deep thought, his fingers tracing patterns on the wooden chair's armrest. "I feel like happiness is always just out of reach," he confessed. "Like it's something I'll get once I achieve enough, earn enough, or become enough."

The old man gave a knowing smile. "Ah, the great lie we all believe—that happiness is something waiting for us in the future." He sighed. "I spent decades chasing it. Told myself I'd be happy once I got my dream job, once I had enough money, once I built a perfect life."

"And did it work?" the young man asked.

The old man shook his head. "No. Because every time I reached a goal, happiness moved further ahead, like a mirage in the desert. There was always something else to achieve, another problem to solve, another reason to postpone happiness."

The young man frowned. "But isn't it natural to want more?"

"Of course," the old man said. "But tell me, if happiness is always tied to something in the future, when will you allow yourself to feel it?"

The young man hesitated. "I don't know."

"That's the problem," the old man said gently. "We tell ourselves that happiness comes after success, after love, after proving something to the world. But what if happiness was never meant to be something we reach? What if it's something we create in how we live every single day?"

The young man thought about his life—about how he had postponed happiness, always thinking, *I'll be happy when...* But what if he could be happy now?

"How do I start?" he asked.

The old man smiled. "By understanding that happiness isn't waiting for you in some perfect future. It's in the way you enjoy a simple meal. In the warmth of a conversation. In the gratitude for what you already have." He paused, looking into the young man's eyes. "Happiness isn't a destination, my boy. It's the way you walk the path."

A quiet realization settled in the young man's heart. He had spent so much time running toward happiness that he had forgotten to experience it.

For the first time, he decided to stop chasing and start living.

Chapter 50: The Final Lesson

The room was filled with the golden light of the setting sun. The old man lay still, his breathing softer now, his voice a whisper of what it once was. The young man sat close, holding his mentor's frail hand, knowing this was the final chapter of their time together.

"You've shared so much with me," the young man said, his voice thick with emotion. "But if there was only one lesson—just one—that you could leave behind, what would it be?"

The old man smiled, a peaceful kind of smile, as if he had already found his answer long ago. He took a slow breath, his gaze fixed on the sky outside the window. "It's simple, my boy. In the end, the only thing that truly matters is how much you loved and how fully you lived."

The young man felt a lump rise in his throat. "But what about success? What about achievements, wealth, and recognition?"

The old man's fingers gave a weak but firm squeeze. "None of that will matter when you take your final breath. No one will care about how much money you made, how many awards you won, or how important the world thought you were. The only thing you will ask yourself is—did I love enough? Did I truly live?"

A deep silence filled the space between them. The young man thought about all the things he had been chasing, the worries that kept him up at night, the endless race to be someone, to achieve something. But now, sitting here, none of that seemed as important as he once believed.

"What does it mean to truly live?" he asked.

The old man's eyes softened. "To wake up each day with gratitude. To give your time to the people who matter. To chase dreams, not because they prove your worth, but because they set your soul on fire. To laugh without holding back, to cry when your heart is heavy, to tell the people you love how much they mean to you."

A tear slipped down the young man's cheek. "And to love?"

"To love," the old man whispered, "is to give without expecting, to forgive even when it's hard, to be present with the ones who need you. Love is the only thing that doesn't fade, even when we're gone."

The young man held his mentor's hand a little tighter, feeling the weight of every word.

The old man smiled again, his eyes filled with the quiet understanding of a life well-lived. "Promise me something," he said.

"Anything," the young man whispered.

"Promise me you won't wait until the end to understand this. Live now. Love now. Because when your time comes, I hope you have no regrets."

The young man nodded, his heart full, his soul changed.

The sun dipped below the horizon, casting the room in soft shadows. The final lesson had been given, and in that moment, the young man understood—this wasn't just a conversation. It was a gift, a guiding light for the road ahead.

And he would carry it with him, always.

Final Words: The Old Man's Last Message

The room was quiet, except for the steady ticking of the old wooden *clock* on the wall. The young man sat beside his mentor, his hands clasped together, his heart heavy with an ache he had never known before.

The old man, his breath shallow, looked at him with tired yet knowing eyes. "If you forget everything I've ever told you, remember this…"

The young man leaned in, afraid to miss a single word.

"We spend our lives chasing—chasing approval, chasing wealth, chasing a future we think will finally make us happy. But in all this chasing, we forget to live."

His voice wavered, but his words were sharp, cutting through the silence. "One day, you'll wake up and realize that the things you worried about didn't matter. That the moments you rushed through were the ones you should have cherished. That the people you assumed would always be there… won't be."

The young man swallowed hard, his vision blurring.

The old man smiled faintly. "Don't wait to say the words that need to be said. Don't waste your life waiting for the 'right time'—because life never pauses. It moves forward, with or without you."

Then, something strange happened.

The *clock* on the wall, which had been ticking steadily all night, suddenly stopped.

No reason. No explanation.

The young man's breath caught in his throat. The silence was so absolute that he could hear his own heartbeat.

The old man noticed it too. His tired gaze flickered toward the *clock*, and for a brief moment, something unreadable crossed his face. But he did not speak of it.

Instead, he whispered, "Time is a gift. Don't waste it."

The young man clenched his fists. "I—I don't want you to go."

The old man gave a weak chuckle. "We all must go, my boy. The only thing that matters is how we lived while we were here."

His eyes softened, but his breath grew weaker. "Promise me…"

The young man leaned closer, his own breath unsteady.

"Promise me that when your time comes, you won't have regrets."

A tear slipped down the young man's face. "I promise."

The old man's lips curled into a faint smile. And then—just like that—he closed his eyes.

The room was silent.

The young man sat still, unable to move. The *clock* remained frozen, its hands forever paused at the moment the old man had spoken his last words.

A shiver ran through him.

The world outside continued as usual. But here, in this quiet room, time itself had bowed in respect.

Conclusion: The Lessons That Remain

The young man stepped outside, feeling the cool air against his face. The world looked the same, yet something within him had shifted.

He had walked into that room as one person and left as another.

The old man's words echoed in his mind—not just as memories, but as truths he could no longer ignore. Life was fragile. Time was fleeting. Regret was the heaviest burden one could carry.

As he walked down the quiet street, he thought of all the things people chase—success, money, recognition—never realizing that the most valuable things are often the ones they overlook. The people they love. The moments they rush through. The simple joys they take for granted.

The old man had left behind no wealth, no empire, no grand legacy. But what he had left was far greater.

He had left wisdom.

And wisdom, the young man realized, had the power to change a life.

He thought about his own life—about the words he had left unsaid, the dreams he had postponed, the love he had held back out of fear. But now, there was no more room for hesitation. No more waiting for 'someday.'

Because *someday* was an illusion.

The young man took a deep breath and made a promise to himself—a promise to live fully, to love deeply, and to leave no words unspoken.

And as he walked forward, a strange sense of peace settled over him.

The old man was gone.

But his lessons would live forever.